# TABLE OF CONTENTS

# ACRONYMS

| | |
|---|---|
| ADP | Army Doctrine Publication |
| ADRP | Army Doctrine Reference Publication |
| AOR | Area of Responsibility |
| CCMD | Combatant Command |
| CRM | Composite Risk Management |
| DOD | Department of Defense |
| HR | House of Representatives |
| NSS | National Security Strategy |
| TC | Training Circular |
| $T_{0-4}$ | Model and Case Study time period designators |
| UCP | Unified Command Plan |

ILLUSTRATIONS

iv

# INTRODUCTION

"I am an American Soldier.
I am a warrior and a member of a team.
I serve the people of the United States, and live the Army Values.
I will always place the mission first.
I will never accept defeat.
I will never quit.
I will never leave a fallen comrade.
I am disciplined, physically and mentally tough, trained and proficient in my warrior tasks and drills.
I always maintain my arms, my equipment and myself.
I am an expert and I am a professional.
I stand ready to deploy, engage, and destroy, the enemies of the United States of America in close combat.
I am a guardian of freedom and the American way of life.
I am an American Soldier."
—approved by Army Chief of Staff Peter Schoomaker, *U.S. Army Soldier's Creed*

The Soldier's Creed and Warrior Ethos hold significant meaning for both American soldiers and the American population. At the root of each is an understanding that the mission always comes first but if a soldier dies, is captured, or is missing in combat then he will be returned honorably to the United States regardless of time and assets required to complete the task. Seemingly, a contradiction exists between these concepts. If the mission is always first, then the soldier never is. However, if a soldier can never leave a fallen comrade behind, then that fallen comrade becomes the mission. It would appear that a soldier might start out secondary to the mission and then potentially become the focus of the mission later.

During unified land operations, the first priority of the command is the successful completion of the military objective, or decisive action, followed by everything else.[1] Furthermore, commanders use prudent risk to ensure mission success when anticipating and

---

[1] Army Doctrine Reference Publication (ADRP) 3-0, *Unified Land Operations*, describes unified land operations as how the Army demonstrates its core competencies of combined arm maneuver and wide area security through decisive action. Decisive action is the concept of continuous, simultaneous offense, defense, stability, or defense support of civil authorities.

1

accepting losses at the strategic, operational, and tactical levels. The individual service member, in turn, is of little significance in the grand scheme. After hostilities end, the priority shifts to maximize every effort to return all fallen, captured, or missing to the United States. However, is this distinction between mission success and individual wellbeing that clear? In modern warfare, does the individual service member hold more strategic value due to the nature of combat? Can the commander truly balance risk by devaluing the individual service member in favor of mission success? What does American doctrine provide to help a commander decide where he can accept risk? What external factors affect the commander's ability to accept risk in a prudent manner? Each of these questions feeds a larger question, are individual service members becoming more strategically important in modern warfare? This study will address this larger question in four sections beginning with a literature review.

The literature review is critical to this study. In it, the reader will find several key definitions central to the argument and detailed discussion of formal works on risk, casualty aversion, the CNN effect, and Warrior Ethos. The definition subsection tackles the concept of the individual. Next, the concept of risk, as defined in national through Army level documentation. The definition of modern warfare follows and explains how it relates to this study. Finally, the definition section finishes with defining strategy and operational art, both imperative to the study. Following the definitions, this monograph reviews writings that focus on risk at multiple echelons within the United States' military framework. From risk, casualty aversion logically flows as a review topic, it is important for the reader to understand the concept as it relates to this study's overall objective. Explaining the importance of mass media and how civilians and military leaders gain understanding through portrayals in the media as to the depth of military actions the population may or may not support is crucial to the study. The literature review section finishes with a review of Warrior Ethos and its effects on civilians and military alike. The methodology section will take these concepts and build upon them to develop a model central to the argument.

The methodology used in this study is a plausibility probe in order to evaluate the developed model in terms of potential validity and value in further analysis.[2] This section discusses a model developed by the author that speaks to the balance a commander must strike between mission success and protection of the soldier. Where that balance exists is where the commander accepts risk to both the mission and the soldier. This section will introduce actors external to the commander that profoundly affect his risk balance. These actors, in combination or individually, exert pressure on the commander as he develops and reacts to mission orders or changes in his operational environment. Depending on where and how much pressure these actors apply determines if the commander has more options, or less, and the correlating increased, or decreased flexibility in how he applies the elements of operational art to achieve the desired strategic end state. The plausibility probe methodology allows the author to show the model has logical merit. Analyzing case studies based on this model help show plausibility in the next section.

The case study section places time as a foundation and are broken in sections overlaid against the model. Framing these five case studies are the Bush administration's initial discussion to go to war in Iraq, circa September 2002, and the transition of sovereignty to the Iraqi government in June 2004. Each case study introduces a build from the previous case that shows change over time. Each case study is structurally similar, starting with an introductory reference for that time period followed with analysis concerning the four critical variables of casualty aversion, public support, political consensus, and mass media position. Each case ends with a discussion as to its plausibility within the bounds of the theory. Each case's plausibility will inform that conclusion.

---

[2] Harry Eckstein, *Regarding Politics: Essays on Political Theory, Stability, and Change* (Berkeley: University of California Press, 1992), 147.

This study finishes with a discussion of the findings for the research question, are individual service members becoming more strategically important in modern warfare? In order to address the question, the judging of the model's plausibility is in order. Also in the conclusion is a rendering on whether or not the doctrine adequately addresses how to account for the impact strategic actors exert on the operational commander. Additionally, the conclusion will contain a discussion of the logical detractions. Finally, the study ends with recommendations for further study and action.

## LITERATURE REVIEW

With an understanding of the context for this study, we can now ask the question; are individuals today more strategically important in modern warfare because the risks to their wellbeing can outweigh the success of the mission? Critical to understanding the research question is the definition of key terms. These key terms are the individual, risk, modern warfare, strategy, and operational art. Isolating the definition of the individual narrows the scope of this research paper necessarily and in so doing, places responsibility for that individual with his commander. As discussed above, risk is the key element for this study. Arguably, it is difficult to measure and may be objectively determined, as stated in both Joint and Army doctrine, but so increasingly significant that a single event may trigger staggering repercussions. Modern warfare must address current and predictable future environments, as opposed to a more common historical definition, in order to frame the study in the real and not theoretical environment. Deriving the definitions for strategy and operational art from joint doctrine ensures application across the force. These definitions are crucial to the research question and ultimately to this study.

### Definitions

For the purpose of this study, the term individual refers to United States service members juxtaposed in time, space, and purpose on a modern battlefield. Additionally, individuals, to include commanders, are able to freely think, respond, form opinions, share opinions, and act singularly on the battlefield.

According to Joint Publication 1-02, *Department of Defense Dictionary of Military and Associated Terms*, risk is the "probability and severity of loss linked to hazards."[3] Specifically, this study focuses on the aspects of risk associated with mission accomplishment and personal risk. Within the scope of risk are two additional concepts that need explanation in order to understand the magnitude of risk and risk decisions. These concepts are prudent risk and acceptable risk. Prudent risk is "deliberate exposure to potential injury or loss when the commander judges the outcome in terms of mission accomplishment as worth the cost."[4] Inherent in this concept is deliberately measuring risk versus reward. A commander should not gamble on a whim or high stakes mission without properly undertaking actions that identify and mitigate the gamble. By undertaking those logical actions, the commander can reasonably assure himself that risks are worth the rewards to the mission. As described in Army Doctrine Reference Publication (ADRP) 5-0, "commanders carefully determine risks, analyze and minimize as many hazards as possible, and then take prudent risks to exploit opportunities."[5]

Acceptable risk is largely an effort by a commander to identify those risks associated with an operation and reduce their number and impact to a level that ensures mission accomplishment without subjecting the unit or members to unnecessary hazards. The Composite

---

[3] U.S. Joint Chiefs of Staff, *Department of Defense Dictionary of Military and Associated Terms*, Joint Publication 1-02 (Washington, DC: U.S. Joint Chiefs of Staff, as amended July 15, 2012), 273.

[4] U.S. Department of the Army, *The Operations Process*, Army Doctrine Reference Publication 5-0 (Washington, D.C.: U.S. Department of the Army, 2012), 4–2.

[5] Ibid., 4–2.

Risk Management (CRM) process is the formal method the commander uses to mitigate risk.[6] "The purpose of the CRM process is to provide a basis for making sound individual and leadership risk decisions. A key element of the risk decision is determination of what constitutes an acceptable level of risk. Risk or potential loss balances against expectations or expected gains. Risk decisions must always be made at the appropriate level of command or leadership based on the level of risk involved."[7] Much like any judgment-based decision, "the assessment of acceptability is largely subjective."[8] Inducing subjectivity into the analysis of risk creates ambiguity in the overall understanding of accepted risk. Given two commanders in similar situations, they may differ completely on what is an acceptable level of risk for their unit and mission. Personality, experience, intellect, and external pressures serve to exacerbate the potential discrepancy in understanding prudent and acceptable risk.

The concept of modern warfare is vast in both time and space. Arguably, it began with the war between Napoleonic France and Hapsburg Austria in 1809 and continues to the present.[9] For the purposes of this study however, this study's definition of modern warfare combines many of the traditional concepts of Dr. Robert Epstein's concept of modern warfare but will take a more adversary-centric tone as described in Army Doctrine Publication (ADP) 3-0. "A hybrid threat is the diverse and dynamic combination of regular forces, irregular forces, terrorist forces,

---

[6] The joint doctrinal term Risk Management replaces the Army doctrinal term Composite Risk Management. However, Army Field Manual 5-19, *Composite Risk Management* continues as a valid reference for the Army when discussing risk management according to *Operational Terms and Military Symbols*, Army Doctrine Reference Publication 1-02.

[7] U.S. Department of the Army, *Composite Risk Management*, Field Manual 5-19 (Washington, D.C.: U.S. Department of the Army, 2006), 1–13.

[8] Ibid., 1–11.

[9] Robert M Epstein, *Napoleon's Last Victory and the Emergence of Modern War* (Lawrence, Kan.: University Press of Kansas, 1994), 6.

criminal elements, or a combination of these forces and elements all unified to achieve mutually benefitting effects. Hybrid threats may involve nation-state adversaries that employ protracted forms of warfare, possibly using proxy forces to coerce and intimidate, or non-state actors using operational concepts and high-end capabilities traditionally associated with nation-states."[10] Training Circular (TC) 7-100 further describes hybrid threat as "the diverse and dynamic combination of regular forces, irregular forces, and/or criminal elements all unified to achieve mutually benefitting effects."[11] The emergence of regular and irregular forces on the battlefield ushered in a more dangerous era for United States military. Arguably, this combination is not new, but technology and the threat's ability to shift between regular and irregular forces to achieve their objective have made them more lethal to general-purpose forces. Additionally, each of these elements will work towards an individual goal while still realizing the overall strategic goal. Regular forces "are governed by international law, military tradition, and custom."[12] Conversely, "irregular forces are unregulated and as a result act with no restrictions on violence or targets for violence."[13] It is important to note that typical Special Forces elements can and often do conduct irregular warfare techniques as part of their doctrine. For this definition, regular forces include the nationally aligned Special Forces elements. This combination serves to pose a viable and dangerous adversary to modern American and allied armed forces.

In this study, strategy is "a prudent idea or set of ideas for employing the instruments of national power in a synchronized and integrated fashion to achieve theater, national, and/or

---

[10] U.S. Department of the Army, *Unified Land Operations*, Army Doctrine Publication 3-0 (Washington, D.C.: U.S. Department of the Army, 2011), 4.

[11] U.S. Department of the Army, *Hybrid Threat*, Training Circular 7-100 (Washington, D.C.: U.S. Department of the Army, 2010), v.

[12] Ibid., v.

[13] Ibid.

multinational objectives."[14] It follows that strategic objectives are goals critical to the success of the operation. Hence, a strategic end state is the culmination of achieved goals from successful operations that meets the commander's desired outcome. Designing and planning the ways and means to achieve the end state is strategy. Similarly, Everett C. Dolman offered strategy is "the link between policy and military action…connects the conduct of war with the intent of politics."[15] Dolman's *Grand Strategy*, "the process by which *all* (emphasis in original) means available to the state are considered in pursuit of a continuing political influence" closely resembles the strategy used for this study. [16] Additionally, B.H. Liddell Hart describes the linkage of the political with the military objectives as "the means to a political end…the military objective should be governed by the political objective, subject to the basic condition that policy does not demand what is militarily – that, is practically – impossible."[17] Each of the theorists would agree that the joint doctrinal definition for strategy effectively conveys the need for the political end to have primacy when forming strategy to which operational art links those political ends to tactical actions.

Operational art is "the cognitive approach by commanders and staffs — supported by their skill, knowledge, experience, creativity, and judgment — to develop strategies, campaigns, and operations to organize and employ military forces by integrating ends, ways, and means."[18] Clearly, to have a successful application of operational art requires commanders and staffs to

---

[14] U.S. Joint Chiefs of Staff, *Department of Defense Dictionary of Military and Associated Terms* (Washington, D.C.: U.S. Joint Chiefs of Staff, 2012), 300.

[15] Everett C Dolman, *Pure Strategy: Power and Principle in the Space and Information Age* (London; New York: Frank Cass, 2005), 6.

[16] Ibid., 26.

[17] Basil Henry Liddell Hart, *Strategy* (New York, N.Y., U.S.A.: Meridian, 1991), 338.

[18] U.S. Joint Chiefs of Staff, *Joint Publication 1-02*, 232.

have superior "skill, knowledge, experience, and judgment" in order to plan and synchronize actions across all levels of warfare towards a single immutable strategic end state. [19] The critical factor for the operational artists is the arrangement of tactical actions. Mission orders and commanders intent statements assign responsibility to subordinate units that assure a clear linkage to the higher headquarters responsibilities and requirements. Doing this at each echelon ensures linkage from strategic to tactical levels of war. In addition, because "operational art applies to all aspects of operations and integrates ends, ways, and means, while accounting for risk," refinement of the linkage of tactical actions to strategic objectives happens from tactical to strategic levels of war. [20] Operational art is the mental gymnastics that creates synergy and cohesive actions across the whole spectrum of modern warfare.

As discussed previously, risk is multi-echeloned and focused on hazard reduction to enable mission accomplishment and to preserve resources. The term infers that each echelon nests risk from strategic to tactical levels of war, similar to operational art integrating ends, ways, and means. Thus, reviewing the Joint and Army doctrine that discusses risk is important to understanding the underlying nature risk plays in the formulation of actions. Additionally, the review of key drivers to this study, casualty aversion in American society, the role media plays in policy formulation and Army ethos is important in understanding how a commander may make a risk decision. The review begins by describing risk as discussed in joint and Army doctrinal manuals. The review transitions to understanding the theory of casualty aversion in American society as it relates to policy. Next is a review of the 'CNN Effect' and its role in national policymaking and strategy. Finally, the review will conclude with a discussion about the effects

_____

[19] U.S. Department of the Army, *Unified Land Operations*, Army Doctrine Reference Publication 3-0 (Washington, D.C.: U.S. Department of the Army, 2012), 4–1.

[20] Ibid., 4–1.

of U.S. Army ethos on decision-making. The literature review will provide the baseline criteria for theory development, evaluating the case studies and conclusions inferred.

## Joint-level risk guidance

Underpinning Joint doctrine is the linkage to national-level leadership through documents that define national interests and goals, such as the *National Security Strategy* (NSS). The national strategic documents and policy decisions from the President form the orders to the Department of Defense for execution of the national security mission. "These documents outline how DOD will support NSS objectives, and provide a framework for other DOD policy and planning guidance."[21] Linking Presidential, Department of Defense, and Joint Staff functions is the *Unified Command Plan* (UCP), developed by the Joint Staff. This document "establishes combatant command (CCMD) missions, responsibilities, and geographic areas of responsibility (AORs)."[22] This guidance provides joint-level leaders parameters for planning operations and a threshold for the amount risk the force may accept are particularly valuable to the study. Operational art is the mechanism by which the joint force links the strategic end state from national leadership and tactical actions in a campaign through time, space, and purpose. Joint-level commanders must address the ends, ways, means, and risk to effectively employ operational art.[23]

In order to account for risk, the Joint force uses the risk management process contained in Joint Publication 3-31, *Command and Control for Joint Land Operations*. "Risk management is a

---

[21] U.S. Joint Chiefs of Staff, *Joint Operations*, Joint Publication 3-0 (Washington, D.C.: U.S. Joint Chiefs of Staff, 2011), I–6.

[22] Ibid.

[23] Ibid., II–4.

function of command and is based on the amount of risk a higher authority is willing to accept."[24]

The process "assists commanders in conserving lives and resources and avoiding or mitigating unnecessary risk, making an informed decision to execute a mission, identifying feasible and effective control measures where specific standards do not exist, and providing reasonable alternatives for mission accomplishment."[25] Joint leaders conduct risk assessments, implement risk mitigation measures, and place command emphasis where necessary to ensure subordinate leaders are aware of the risks inherent in the operation. The Joint process serves to link the national leadership's view of risk to that of the operation. The Army narrows that focus to the warfighter-level, specifically as it pertains to mission accomplishment and soldier safety.

## Army-level risk guidance

For the United States Army, risk to mission and personnel takes on a much more tangible meaning. The nature of warfare addressed in Army doctrine is at the point of the explosion, rifle fire, hand-to-hand combat, and base human survival instincts. Of course, over years of professionalization, the Army established doctrinal constructs to sharpen unit leadership, unity of effort, and morale, which are all necessary to accomplish the mission. The Army uses three primary documents to provide guidance and direction when discussing risk. The first document is *The Army Posture Statement of 2012*, which establishes the Army's priorities and guidelines for the upcoming year.[26] The second document is Army Doctrine Reference Publication 3-0, *Unified*

---

[24] U.S. Joint Chiefs of Staff, *Command and Control for Joint Land Operations*, Joint Publication 3-31 (Washington, D.C.: U.S. Joint Chiefs of Staff, 2010), IV–13.

[25] Ibid., IV–13.

[26] John M. McHugh and Raymond T. Odierno, "2012 U.S. Army Posture Statement," *U.S. Department of the Army*, February 17, 2012, https://secureweb2.hqda.pentagon.mil/VDAS_ArmyPostureStatement/2012/ (accessed November 16, 2012).

*Land Operations*, which provides "overarching guidance on unified land operations and the Army's core competencies of combined arms maneuver and wide area security…it accounts for the uncertain and ever-changing nature of operations and recognizes that military operations are foremost a human undertaking."[27] The third document that undergirds Army guidance and direction on risk is Army Doctrine Reference Publication 5-0, *The Operations Process.* This document discusses the concept of prudent risk and the Army's risk management process. Each of these documents serves to shape how the Army fights, trains, and wins.

*The Army Posture Statement 2012* establishes the strategic context for the coming year. In this regard, the Army faces a significant transition from a war footing to an Army coming home. As the Army transitions home, fiscal challenges and a degraded global economy will affect the "transition to a smaller yet capable force fully prepared to conduct the full range of operations worldwide."[28] This force expects to prevent, shape, and win in future conflicts while shrinking in size, but not in the traditional dangerous manner where leadership and experience bleed off precipitously.[29] The nation exposes itself to strategic, operational, and tactical risk when reducing the size and scope of the force with little regard to the impending strategic environment. This document serves to acknowledge the need to reduce the size of the Army but not to such a degree where the Army cannot prevent, shape, or win. The coming year will set the conditions for the Army of 2020, a force that has "a versatile mix of capabilities, formations and equipment that is lethal, agile, adaptable and responsive."[30] With the guideline to future endeavors proposed in *The*

---

[27] Ibid.

[28] Ibid.

[29] Ibid.

[30] Ibid.

*Army Posture Statement 2012*, it is the role of doctrine to outline specific actions necessary to account for and mitigate risks to mission and personnel.

"Risk, uncertainty, and chance are inherent in all military operations."[31] The Army Doctrine Reference Publication 3-0, *Unified Land Operations*, painstakingly describes risk in a three-paragraph section that describes why a commander must assume risk, the necessity to intelligently evaluate risk, and the benefits of decisively accepting risk. The commander's role is important for when they "accept risk, they create opportunities to seize, retain, and exploit the initiative and achieve decisive results."[32] Willingly embracing risk can lead to boldness and initiative that affords a commander the ability to exploit an enemy's weakness to the advantage of the Army. Boldness and initiative are powerful tools for a commander but "inadequate planning and preparation recklessly risks forces."[33] Commanders are equipped with staffs and experience that allows them to understand and visualize the situation and act boldly and with initiative, not carelessly. The experienced commanders can "balance audacity and imagination with risk and uncertainty to strike at a time and place and in a manner wholly unexpected by enemy forces."[34] These commanders "create and maintain the conditions necessary to seize, retain, and exploit the initiative and achieve decisive results."[35] Balancing risk to the force and with a desired end state and minimizing hazards to friendly forces allows a commander to empower subordinates with initiative and flexibility in order to achieve the desired results of the plan. *Unified Land Operations* seeks to empower commanders with discretion and initiative when formulating plans

---

[31] U.S. Department of the Army, *Army Doctrine Reference Publication 3-0*, 4–9.

[32] Ibid., 4–9.

[33] Ibid.

[34] Ibid.

[35] Ibid.

of action, allowing them the opportunity to "seize, retain, and exploit the initiative and achieve decisive results."[36]

The Army Doctrine Reference Publication 5-0, *The Operations Process*, "provides an expanded discussion of planning, preparing, executing, and assessing operations" and coupled with an understanding of unified land operations arms commanders with tools to accept and mitigate risks to their unit. The doctrine identifies risk management, a "process of identifying, assessing, and controlling risks arising from operational factors and making decisions that balance risk cost with mission benefits."[37] As discussed in the introduction to this section, prudent risk is central to developing the plan that achieves the objective. A commander must make a deliberate decision to assume risk and where and to whom that risk is placed. The process of risk management allows the commander to "identify and mitigate risks associated with all hazards that have the potential to injure or kill friendly and civilian personnel, damage or destroy equipment, or otherwise impact mission effectiveness."[38] The process is composed of five steps, identify hazards, assess hazards to determine risks, develop controls and make risk decisions, implement controls, and supervise and evaluate.[39] It is critical that all staffs and subordinate leaders incorporate risk management and make recommendations accordingly. A graphical depiction of this balance is shown in Figure 1. The commander, with the help of his staff, understands the importance of the mission and the necessity to preserve his resources for future operations. In this capacity, he must balance husbanding resources (individuals) and using the appropriate amount of aggression to achieve his mission. Where this balance exists is solely up to

---

[36] Ibid.

[37] U.S. Department of the Army, *Army Doctrine Reference Publication 5-0*, iii, 1–12.

[38] Ibid., 1–12.

[39] Ibid.

the commander's discretion and based on his training, his understanding of doctrine,

professionalism, and his experience. This is a personal decision for the commander to make.

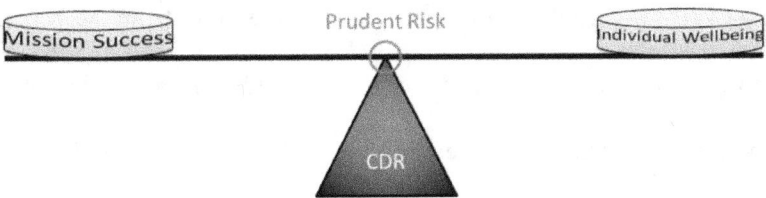

Figure 1: Author's representation of the prudent risk balance commander's must strike between mission success and individual based on current doctrine.

*Source:* Created by the author.


Risk must have the commander's attention so that balance between mission and costs gain the

necessary analysis to achieve the mission without gambling on results.

In evaluating the literature surrounding risk, the overarching conclusion is that risk needs

proper accounting and mitigation to ensure success. At the national level of government, leaders

measure risk in terms of conflict deterrence or policy advancement. There is precious little

attention given to the discussion of risk to mission or personnel or the linkage to the operational

environment. Army-level guidance begins to address the specifics of risk to mission and

personnel and describes mechanisms to balance mission, soldiers, and cost. All of the literature

describes the necessity to ensure plans and end states nest through the echelons of command, but

there is little discussion of nested risks. Although the Army-level guidance describes the need to

ensure communication between elements about risk decisions, there is no formal discussion as to

how to accomplish that. Many references describe initiative in meeting the commander's intent,

but initiative to take risk is more ambiguous. Having discussed the concept of modern warfare,

clearly the adversary will seek to place individuals and missions at risk to ensure a strategic

victory while purposefully giving up the tactical victory. Are our tactical level leaders assuming risk that inextricably links to strategic aims while the strategic leaders are unaware their aims are at risk of failure?

No review of risk is complete without reviewing the input from the timeless military theoretician, Carl von Clausewitz. Clausewitz is well studied and regarded in the present day modern warfare period. He wrote about uncertainty and the degree to which it affected operations in his era.[40] For Clausewitz, uncertainty is monumentally difficult and only increases as the level of war increases. Risk and uncertainty abound due to the nature of warfare as a human endeavor. Humans, in their exceedingly unpredictable nature create an environment for war that makes it "the most complex of human undertakings and filled with unknowns."[41] Clausewitz mentions the terms chance and luck in his writings when discussing uncertainty and its counter, genius. He also uses analogies and metaphors to further describe the nature of warfare and risk. To counter risk and uncertainty required an unmatched intellect that "retains some glimmerings of the inner light which leads to truth; and second, the courage to follow this faint light wherever it may lead."[42] Clausewitz termed these qualities as genius, developed through careful and thorough study, not genetically preordained.[43]

---

[40] Carl von Clausewitz, *On War*, ed. Michael Howard and Peter Paret (Princeton, N.J.: Princeton University Press, 1984), 178, 586.

41 J. Boone Bartholomees and Army War College (U.S.). Strategic Studies Institute, *U.S. Army War College Guide to National Security Issues* (Carlisle, Pa.: Strategic Studies Institute, U.S. Army War College, 2008), 67, http://purl.access.gpo.gov/GPO/LPS95737 (accessed November 6, 2012).

42 Clausewitz, *On War*, 102.

43 Ibid., 100–112.

Casualty Aversion

Casualty aversion in American society does not exist as a planning consideration in military actions. Instead, the myth that the American population is casualty averse exists and is pervasive. In fact, the public is more permissive about accepting casualties in war than both national and military leaders understand. The amount of aversion by the population depends on the amount of consensus-based leadership provided by national and military leaders.[44] The American public understands and seeks consensus from national leadership. When they witness consensus amongst leaders and receive adequate explanations of the policy, the people show surprisingly more tolerance for casualties than the policy makers believed possible.[45] Consensus between the Executive and Legislative branches of U.S. civilian leadership is critical; the general public has become less and less attuned to when and for what reason military forces may be used and therefore more reliant on these institutions to inform them on policy. In particular, "when political leaders fail to agree on the benefits and costs of a prospective or ongoing military operation, there should be little surprise that the public also becomes divided."[46] Higher echelons of leadership perceive the sustainment of casualties as fear or reticence on the part of the public. Senior policy makers and military decision makers seemingly, perhaps from the Vietnam-syndrome, believe that Americans absolutely abhor the thought of casualties to the degree that

44 Richard A. Lacquement, Jr., "The Casualty-Aversion Myth," *Naval War College Review* 57, no. 1 (Winter 2004): 42.

45 Ibid., 51.

46 Timothy F. Bishop and Army War College (U.S.), *A Nation At War: Combat Casualties and Public Support*, USAWC strategy research project (Carlisle Barracks, Pa: U.S. Army War College, 2008), 6, http://handle.dtic.mil/100.2/ADA478483 (accessed November 8, 2012).

they design a "strategy that specifically cites casualty aversion" to justify the use of force. [47] Casualty aversion exists, but where specifically.

According to Dr. Richard A. Lacquement, there are five major manifestations of casualty aversion in American society. The first is the "Vietnam syndrome" that describes how Americans are hard pressed to accept military expeditions abroad due to the experiences of the Vietnam War. The second, Senator John Glenn's "Dover Test" that describes the negative affect on the American populace of flagged draped coffins returning from war. The third is the "CNN Effect" that suggests the American people will not stomach horrific near-real time images of casualties beamed back to their living rooms. Fourth, the question/test of the Weinberger/Powell Doctrine and how it relates to the support of the American people and Congress before attempting military action. Next is "post-heroic warfare" that asserts the American people can no longer tolerate the quantities of casualties that results from a conventional clash of armies. Finally, the American people are averse to casualties due to the underrepresentation of civil elites in the armed forces. Each of these explanations for casualty aversion in American society has proven empirically false. It is the myth of these that tends to affect the leadership in an averse manner. [48]

Lacquement further argues that there are four major negative effects of this mythical view of public casualty aversion. The first is the inefficient and ineffective application of military action. The second is the apparent emboldening of our enemies when aversion exists. The third is the substitution of technology for manpower. The last reason is the failure of military leaders to provide unbiased and timely military advice to policy makers. Each of these serves to promulgate the myth further.

---

[47] Ibid., 4.

[48] Lacquement, Jr., "The Casualty-Aversion Myth," this paragraph is a summation of Dr. Lacquement's argument as to his main assertions on American casualty aversion.

The first negative effect is this misrepresentation leads to inefficient and ineffective execution of the military action.[49] This occurs when both national and military leaders believe the public will not stand casualties and therefore unnecessarily limit the aggressiveness or scope of a military action to ensure casualties remain low. Compounding the danger of this high-level risk aversion is the emphasis or pressure placed on junior leaders and soldiers to conduct operations using low-risk methods. Each of these examples serves to demonstrate that a false assumption of the tolerance for casualties drives a military action in a less than efficient/effective manner.

When the appearance of casualty aversion exists, it tends to expand past American borders. Adversaries see this weakness and seek to exploit it.[50] These same adversaries will use casualty aversion to strengthen their position globally, as well as sew doubt into the minds of potential U.S. allies or coalition partners. A typical propaganda piece from Al Qaeda would assure the world that when the U.S. suffered casualties, they would quickly retreat. The evidence provided are the past impressions from American reactions to events such as the Lebanon Embassy bombing and the quick mission transition in Somalia after the deaths of eighteen American soldiers. All attributed to the impression that Americans are casualty averse.

The seemingly traditional American pursuit of technology as a substitute for manpower serves to expose soldiers less, but may not be the best tool for the job.[51] Arguably, there is value in technological innovation, but technology or standoff weapon capabilities cannot replace the soldier when taking and occupying terrain is required. Additionally, this ill-founded pursuit to limit casualties for fear of public backlash drives weapons procurement. Building a weapon around casualty aversion risks building the wrong weapon, one that will not meet the needs on the

---

[49] Ibid., 44–47.

[50] Ibid., 47–48.

[51] Ibid., 49.

battlefield where war is a human and not technological endeavor. Exposing soldiers to risk is a fundamental leadership challenge taught in all leader development schools.[52] Soldiers that embody the Warrior Ethos can act honorably and professionally to an ill-structured problem; a missile or shell launched from miles away cares little about honor.[53]

Another negative effect is when military leaders fail or hesitate to recommend the use of military power based on the perception of its cost in casualties.[54] A belief that the American public will not stomach American casualties is not the purview of the military leader, he should only serve to weigh costs to benefits and recommend the best course of action from the military perspective. Military leaders that use casualty aversion to argue against a military option for national leaders are doing a disservice and risking their military ethic. The weight of what the American people can bear is in the realm of the political leadership.

American national and military leaders must understand the dynamic of public opinion and their views towards casualties in order to understand the range of options available to them. According to Lacquement, leadership serves to widen the realm of the possible in respect to casualties for the American people.[55] If leaders agree and dissention is limited, the American people tend to provide ample support for military actions and the resulting casualties. Conversely, if dissent reigns, the American people stomach less military action and fewer casualties.[56] When leaders overemphasize casualty aversion in society, accurately calculating the costs and benefits

---

[52] U.S. Department of the Army, *The Army*, Field Manual 1 (Washington, D.C.: U.S. Department of the Army, 2005), 1–19.

[53] Ibid., 1–18.

[54] Lacquement, Jr., "The Casualty-Aversion Myth," 49–50.

[55] Ibid., 50–51.

[56] Ibid., 51.

is near impossible. This leads to risk averse behavior and failure in policy. The American people understand that to achieve policy objectives some risks are necessary, so long as the leadership shows consensus, provides an explanation, and are willing to do so.

Casualty aversion exists in American society, but not just with the American people. The role of leadership, national and military, determines the extent to which the American people will accept military action and the resultant casualties. When leaders are unsure of or unwilling to follow a less desirable course, the myth of casualty aversion is a heavy bargaining tool to achieve their desires. However, using casualty aversion as a planning assumption unnecessarily limits the realm of policy options available to leaders. Weighing heavily on the minds of these leaders are the ever increasing and dramatic images broadcast globally from warzones far from home.

CNN Effect and media

The CNN Effect is the concept that dramatic images broadcast nearly simultaneously to homes in the United States have immediate public demand for action.[57] The existence of the effect is debatable across the spectrum of leadership, journalism, and scholars.[58] As with casualty aversion, research and literature describes the CNN Effect as a function of leadership and understanding. Robert MacNeil describes the relationship between media and leadership as necessary, but the leader has the upper hand if he can successfully articulate and drive foreign policy. He states in his article, "Television however lurid, responsible, or irresponsible will not drive foreign policy. When he [the leader] fails to do so, it [media] may."[59] The added difficulty

---

[57] Bernard W. Kasupski, III., "CNN Effect: A Direct Path to the American Center of Gravity?" (Newport, Rhode Island: U.S. Naval War College, 2000), 1.

[58] Eytan Gilboa, "Global Television News and Foreign Policy: Debating the CNN Effect," *International Studies Perspectives* 6, no. 3 (August 2005): 335, http://doi.wiley.com/10.1111/j.1528-3577.2005.00211.x (accessed November 16, 2012).

[59] Robert L Snyder and Everette E Dennis, *Media & Public Life* (New Brunswick [etc.]:

21

is that the media is wholly capable of creating influence where political and military leadership does not wish it to exist. The design of storylines, articles, and visuals are to elicit an emotional response within the individual.[60] The individuals form groups and soon the group is large enough to shape policy or opinion. The CNN Effect may not force policy makers to a decision, but may clearly pressure decision makers into a foreign policy decision or create enough of a subconscious impact on decision makers to influence a decision where it normally would not.[61]

Clearly, leaders at all levels of war carefully consider the role of media on the modern battlefield, personally, and professionally. Tactical images broadcast globally have strategic implications, which ensure that operational commanders are completely aware of the media and how it shapes public perception, policy, and future operations. Army Doctrine Reference Publication 3-0 discusses the importance of media as it relates to informing and influencing which is the "integration of designated information-related capabilities in order to synchronize themes, messages, and actions with operations to inform United States and global audiences, influence foreign audiences, and affect adversary and enemy decision-making."[62] The manual further clarifies the importance of media to soldiers and leaders, arguing that the adversary may use each American misstep or loss of professionalism as propaganda through the global media.[63] Coupled with the myth of casualty aversion, national and military leaders must attempt to guard

---

Transaction, 1997), 123.

[60] Frank J. Stech, "Winning CNN Wars," *Parameters*, n.d., http://www.carlisle.army.mil/usawc/Parameters/Articles/1994/stech.htm (accessed November 16, 2012).

[61] Gilboa, "Global Television News and Foreign Policy," 336.

[62] U.S. Department of the Army, *Army Doctrine Reference Publication 3-0*, 3–3.

[63] Ibid., 1–14.

against the media shaping or informing their opinion, the public's opinion, and then foreign policy, whether by risk aversion or media manipulation.

## United States Army Warrior Ethos

According to Christopher Coker, warrior ethos is described "as the foundation of a soldier's total commitment to victory, it encourages the soldier to put the mission first and refuse to admit defeat. It is designed to equip soldiers with courage and to remind all service members what is expected of them and what they should expect of each other. This is 'down and dirty' stuff, not high-tech, and it is distinctly 'old-fashioned.'[64] Additionally, the warrior ethos speaks to a sacred code, honor, a sense of community, and family with trust as its cornerstone.[65] The ethos bonds individual warriors to each other, it bonds groups of soldiers together, and it binds these warriors to the citizenry of the nation. Fighting for each other and unit cohesion are the "primary" combat motivators, but soldiers also consider "moral and ideological motivators such as liberation, freedom, and democracy" when war arises.[66] When a member acts without honor, it is felt throughout the entire community. There are norms and mores that dictate behaviors and account for uncertainty depending on the community, but the warrior community is responsible for self-policing the battlefield to ensure warfare remains "a moral activity."[67] The elements of warrior ethos described by Coker are similar to the United States Army's Warrior Ethos as depicted in the Army's Capstone doctrinal manual.

---

[64] Christopher Coker, *The Warrior Ethos: Military Culture and the War on Terror* (London; New York: Routledge, 2007), 132–133.

[65] Ibid., 135.

[66] John S Brown, *Kevlar Legions : The Transformation of The U.S. Army, 1989-2005* (Washington, D.C.: Center of Military History United States Army, 2011), 279, http://purl.fdlp.gov/GPO/gpo16049 (accessed November 6, 2012).

[67] Coker, *The Warrior Ethos*, 144.

The US Army Warrior Ethos embedded in the Soldier's Creed as four declarative statements that define the very essence of an American soldier: *I will always place the mission first. I will never accept defeat. I will never quit. I will never leave a fallen comrade.*[68] These simple statements have profound meaning to the American soldier. They set the conditions that establish the "selfless commitment to the Nation, mission, unit, and fellow Soldiers that all Soldiers espouse."[69] Central to internalizing the ethos is the professionalism in the organization. This sense of professionalism creates the environment where each and every soldier understands the impossibility of accepting "failure and instead overcome all obstacles with honor" and "fight through all conditions to victory, no matter how long it takes and how much effort is required."[70] Unlike citizens, soldiers swear or affirm to defend the Constitution. This commitment to the nation and subsequently to the Army shows "their commitment to the Army's guiding values and standards by willingly performing their duty at all times and subordinating their personal welfare to that of others without expecting reward or recognition."[71] Institutionalizing the ethos ensures soldiers will always fight for each other, die for each other, and support one another in all endeavors. It creates the sense of family and kinship that distinguishes them starkly from the citizen. Soldiers will always place the mission before themselves, they will never accept defeat, and they will never quit, and will never leave a fallen comrade behind.

The warrior ethos embodied by the American soldier is critical to the success of the Army in any endeavor. As discussed previously, this ethos serves to bind individuals to each other, to groups, and to the American citizen through honor. These soldiers are citizens and are

---

[68] U.S. Department of the Army, *Field Manual 1*, 1–16.

[69] Ibid.

[70] Ibid., 1–18.

[71] Ibid.

24

willing to fight for the causes of the nation, a behavior that is not prevalent throughout all of society. "Cohesion, or the strong emotional bonds between soldiers" drive this behavior, a willingness to fight for each other not some ethereal sense of democracy or other such calling.[72] Through leadership from the highest levels to smallest cohesive unit, the Army espouses professionalism, honor, and duty, which instill a sense of real trust within the profession, and it is "because our soldiers trust the Army as an institution, they now look to the Army to provide the moral direction for war."[73] These linkages and bonds from soldier to soldier, leader to soldier or soldier to unit establishes fellowship that is critical to success on the modern battlefield. Faith and trust in comrades and institutional values that forge honor enable unit effectiveness and achieve mission success. The Army learns lessons from prior experiences and in so doing has ensured that "there would be no pictures of jubilant insurgents dancing on a helicopter, no American bodies dragged through the streets, no captured materials, and no hostages" in future wars, so long as ethos and professionalism remain.[74]

The question, grounded in the context for this study; has the risk to individuals made them more strategically important in modern warfare because American doctrine inadequately addresses risk? As discussed previously, risk is multi-echeloned and focused on hazard reduction or avoidance for mission accomplishment or personal danger. The term infers that each echelon nests risk from strategic to tactical levels of war, similar to operational art integrating ends, ways, and means at these echelons. The review of the joint and Army doctrine established risk as important to understanding the underlying nature it plays in the formulation of actions.

---

[72] Leonard Wong and Army War College (U.S.). Strategic Studies Institute, *Why They Fight: Combat Motivation in the Iraq War* ([Carlisle Barracks, PA]: Strategic Studies Institute, U.S. Army War College, 2003), 23.

[73] Ibid., 23.

[74] Brown, *Kevlar Legions*, 424.

Additionally, the review of key drivers to this study, casualty aversion in American society, public support for the cause, the role the media plays in policy formulation and the consensus among senior strategic leaders shows how a commander may have to alter a risk decision based on these pressures. Observing these products in a theoretical model may provide insight into the balance operational commanders must strike between accomplishing the mission and soldier wellbeing, and the degree these individuals are of increasingly strategic importance.

## METHODOLOGY

This monograph uses the plausibility probe methodology in order to evaluate the developed model in terms of potential validity and value in further analysis.[75] As this particular construct of a plausibility probe is untested and developed by the author based on doctrinal understanding of risk, warrior ethos, casualty aversion, public support, political consensus, and the role of media in policy decisions, it is best to evaluate it against historical perspectives for evidence of validity. A plausibility probe analysis allows for a comparative study of the cases to validate or refute the validity of the theoretical construct. The model itself is developed from an amalgamation of various related topics discussed in the Literature Review section of this study that when aggregated create a new model on the impacts of external influences to the operational commander's risk decision.

The model introduced in this study describes the balance a commander must strike between mission success and protection of the soldier. Where that balance exists is where the commander accepts risk to both the mission and the soldier, previously defined as prudent risk. In a vacuum, that balance would naturally fall in the exact middle of the scale where the commander assures mission success and reasonably ensures the survival and protection of soldiers. The

---

[75] Eckstein, *Regarding Politics*, 147.

commander attains this balance through his own exposure and understanding of doctrine, training received (as a recipient or instructor), understanding of his profession (leadership roles and responsibilities, soldier roles and responsibilities, and ethos), and his experiences (personal or otherwise). This balance affords the commander options in how he applies operational art to the mission. In a central position on the scale, the commander has flexibility and can apply the elements of operational art, but his choices and methods are not limitless (Figure 2).

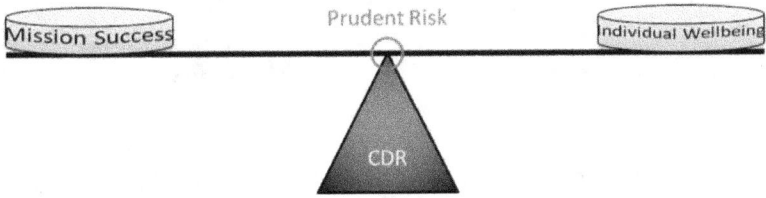

Figure 2: Prudent risk in balance.

*Source:* Created by the author.

If the commander deems that he can assume more risk with the soldier and apply more weight to mission acceptance, he can move the balance point left towards the more heavily weighted mission in order to achieve balance, which will provide more options by which he can accomplish the mission (Figure 3).

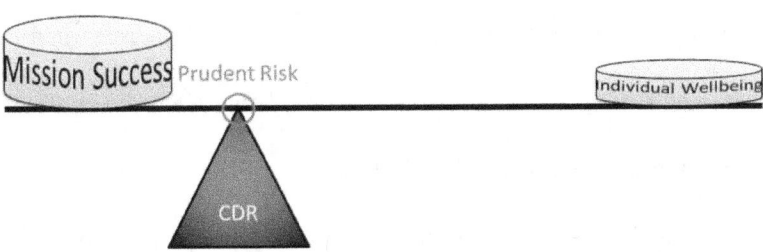

Figure 3: Prudent risk balance weighted towards mission success and assumed risk on the individual.

*Source:* Created by the author.

Conversely, if the commander believes that his resources (soldiers) are limited and he must preserve them more aggressively, he may assume risk with mission accomplishment (short term) in order to preserve his soldiers, which will limit his options in applying operational art to the mission (Figure 4).

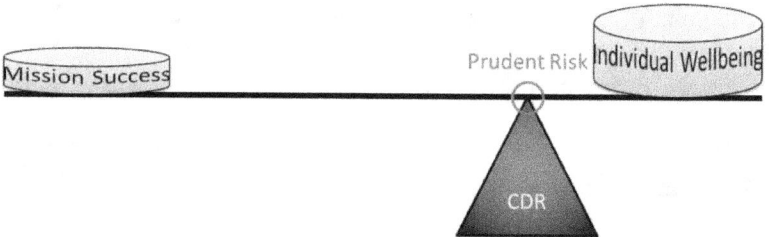

Figure 4: Prudent risk balance weighted towards the individual and assumed risk on mission success.

*Source:* Created by the author.

In this model, the commander who has sole control over the amount of flexibility in applying operational art and it is he alone who decides what has more importance, the mission or the soldier. Current Army doctrine sufficiently familiarizes the commander with his role in this process.

However, the commander is never in a vacuum and is constantly under pressure or influence when deciding the fate of the mission and his soldiers. Superior to and externally generated pressures from strategic actors conspire to unbalance what the commander achieved. For this model, the strategic actors consist of the Executive Branch political leadership, Legislative Branch political leadership, the media (generally lumped, not necessarily in conglomeration), and the general public citizen. The strategic actors influence one another through various mechanisms (political statements, media stories, congressional hearings, or speeches) on a myriad of topics. In this case, of note the topic is military operations and the level of risk acceptable at this strategic level (Figure 5).

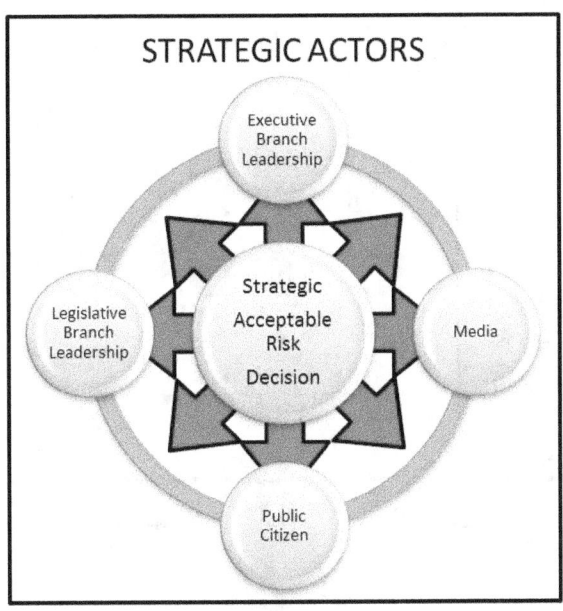

Figure 5: Strategic actors exert pressures internally that drive the level of acceptable risk for military operations.

*Source:* Created by the author.

Each of these actors has an agenda, some in line with others and some in opposition. The system of strategic actors viewed similarly to a bubble level with each actor applying weight to their edge, dragging the bubble away from center. This process is continuous and ever changing with the snapshot outcome driving the amount of pressure applied to the operational commander in terms of where to balance risk, mission or soldier. These pressures measured in terms of casualty aversion, public support, consensus between Executive and Legislative political leadership, and the "media" position on the issue drive the amount of strategically acceptable risk, which then exerts force on the balanced risk scale of the operational commander (Figure 6).

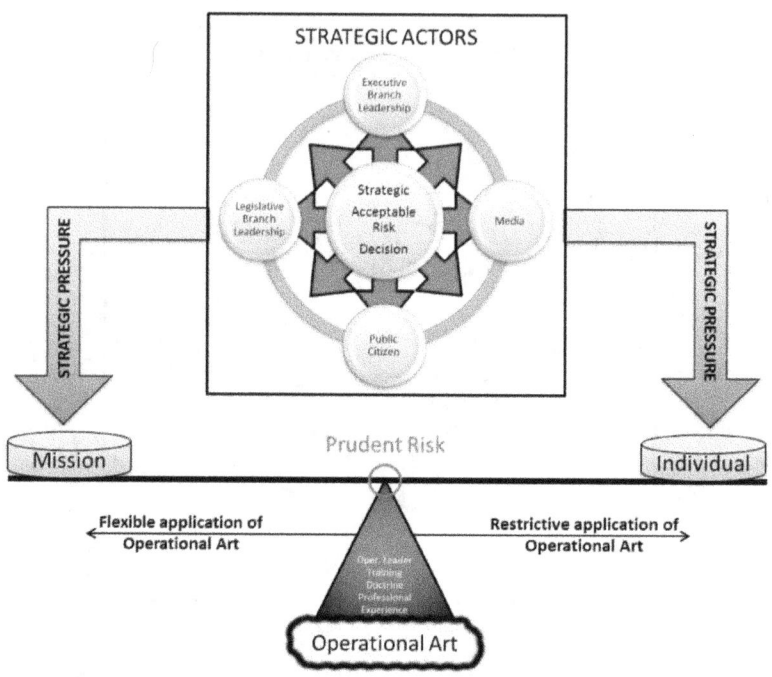

Figure 6: Application of pressure from strategic actors on the operational commander's *professional* risk decision after his training, understanding of doctrine, professionalism, and experience combine to inform his decision, arbitrarily forcing movement to counteract that additional weight.

*Source:* Created by the author.

This force/pressure may drive the operational commander to re-balance his prudent risk either towards mission or towards the individual. Accrediting this phenomenon to simply "following orders" provided by superiors is easy, but in the midst of linking tactical actions to strategic goals in time, space, and purpose (operational art) creates an unanticipated change that the commander and his staff are ill prepared to integrate into the current plan. Arguably, this challenge is more painful if these strategic actors unwittingly change the strategic end state.

This model cannot divorce itself from time. In any snapshot of time, there will likely be some form of imbalance between mission accomplishment and the individual's wellbeing. It is the strategic actor, through mission orders that supplies the catalyst for imbalance that the commander must attempt to put back in balance. As conflict progresses over time, looking at a single risk decision or change in mission does not adequately show the interaction of variables in that risk decision. Figure 9 depicts a model for the outbreak thorough completion of the conflict used in this study and what the author hypothesizes is a visual for balancing risk decisions according to doctrine.

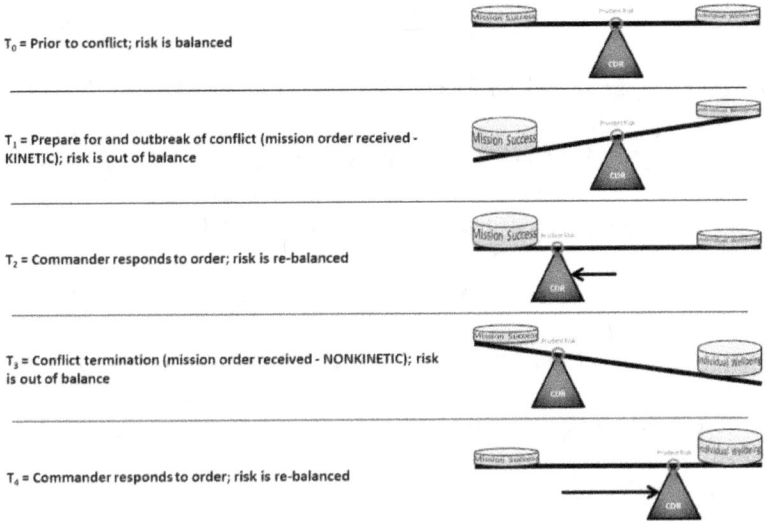

Figure 7: Time-phased model for how commanders re-balance risk following a mission change. *Source:* Created by the author.

Time Zero ($T_0$) is the steady state pre-conflict conditions that exist in a garrison non-deployed environment. The commander is concerned about risk as it is associated with training events and normal life events. He balances this risk through the risk management process outlined earlier.

Time One ($T_1$) shows the imbalance created for the commander when political leadership determines that conflict is necessary and the unit postures on a war footing. The commander now deals with an imbalance to his risk decision, no longer is he concerned about normal life events and training, but is concerned about how to accomplish the assigned mission. This period is the only one that has any reasonable characteristics shared with current doctrine that addresses where the commander and staff can look to identify and mitigate immediate threats to life and mission.

Time Two ($T_2$) reflects the commander's decisions that re-balance the added emphasis on mission accomplishment with the wellbeing of his soldiers. With added emphasis on mission accomplishment, the commander is freer to take risk and has more options available when applying the elements of operational art to satisfy the political end state. The conditions exist where citizens are not averse to casualties (within reason), public support is strong for the military mission, the Executive and Legislative Branches are in consensus about the use of the military option, and the mass media is in support of the action. In general, the preponderance of the strategic actors supports the military option. With little counter argument from strategic actors, the commander is able to identify prudent risk as if he were in a vacuum in accordance with how the ambiguous doctrine defines for him.

Time Three ($T_3$) denotes a shift in the mission from predominately kinetic to stability focused, whereas the traditional mission is accomplished and now "mop up" operations or stability operations begin. Several reasons may cause this shift; in this case, conflict termination will suffice. Because the political leadership determined that the need for kinetic military operations is no longer required, the emphasis moves to the individual's wellbeing, in other words to bring the soldiers home heroically. The commander's risk decision is again out of balance and must be reconciled to ensure he meets the desires of the strategic end state articulated by the political leadership. In this period, the ambiguous nature of the current doctrine helps the commander little. The strategic actors are able and do exert influence on his risk equation.

Time Four ($T_4$) depicts the decisions the commander must make in order to re-balance with the added emphasis on the individual. No longer is the commander as free to assume risk to the soldier, he must preserve them. Strategic actors have determined that the risk to the individual is greater than the risk to the mission and the commander is limited in his options to accomplish

32

the military mission. The commander remains burdened by military objectives, but he must now take more care in how he employs his units and the soldiers to meet the end state. He is more restricted in how he employs the elements of operational art when linking tactical tasks with strategic objectives in time, space, and purpose, but in his restriction has re-balanced the risk decision. Understanding time in this model is critical to the model presented and better shows how risk decisions levied on a commander and his resultant efforts to re-balance that risk between mission accomplishment and the individual soldier's wellbeing.

To test the plausibility of this model, the study must identify the independent and dependent variables to show a potential causal relationship as per the parameters of the plausibility probe methodology.[76] For this study, the independent variable is the political discourse and interaction among the strategic actors attempting to establish the strategic risk acceptance threshold with casualty aversion, public support, consensus, and media position as the products of that discourse which directs, pressures, or influences the commander to adjust his risk decision. The dependent variable is the balance point struck between mission accomplishment and individual wellbeing and prudent risk. There are adequate measures for the independent variable in this study, other than to acknowledge the existence through occurrences. The dependent variable takes place when there is evidence that alterations to operational military actions follow the alteration of the independent variable.

The author will operationalize the variables as follows. The independent variable, the interaction between the strategic actors introduced in this study and quite plausibly, this interaction will cause a change in pressure applied to the operational commander's risk equation. For this study, defining the variables will enable better understanding and better show the existence of a plausible relationship between the independent variables and the dependent

---

[76] Ibid., 151.

variable. The first measureable product of the independent variable is casualty aversion, more importantly is its perceived existence and to what extent. The main method of measuring casualty aversion is through reputable polling returns conducted nationally and in a logical frequency inquiring as to whether the war is a favorable option and whether the war is worth the effort. The second product is public support for military actions. The method for measuring this variable is by viewing the mounting deaths from combat combined with the public's impression of the progress made towards achieving the objectives articulated to them by national leaders, again gleaned from national polling.[77] The same level of reputation and frequency are imperative to show plausibility in causality. The third product is consensus levels within the leadership. For this study, consensus means that Executive and Legislative Branch leaders agree on the course chosen or advocated with little to no dissent. Also for this study, senior military leadership and the President are in consensus with no outward public dissent. This study will not address private dissent between the Executive Branch and the senior military leadership. More importantly, consensus between Executive and Legislative Branches is the better measure for this variable gained through voting records, which will form the preponderance of occurrences that will show consensus. The final product is the mass media's general espoused position on the use of military action. Mass media traditionally consists of the amalgamation of print, video, and internet news sources designed to reach large audiences, for this case study, television news is the source for measuring media position.[78] An overall general coverage of combat operations (minutes devoted) and volume of stories involving Iraq (minutes devoted) subjected to citizens will measure mass

---

[77] Christopher Gelpi, Peter D. Feaver, and Jason Reifler, "Success Matters: Casualty Sensitivity and the War in Iraq," *International Security* 30, no. 3 (December 1, 2005): 7–46, http://www.jstor.org/stable/4137486 (accessed December 3, 2012).

[78] S.E. Smith, "What is Mass Media?," *wiseGEEK*, n.d., http://www.wisegeek.com/what-is-mass-media.htm (accessed November 14, 2012).

media's position on military action using the three most popular television news media outlets as sources, ABC, CBS, and NBC.[79] The bias of the stories is immaterial to the study as it is debatable whether or not adults are swayed one way or the other based on the message delivered or whether there is trust in the truthfulness of the media in particular.[80] However, the connotation is important, each media section will look at how positive or negative the media is portraying stories.

Using the plausibility probe methodology in order to evaluate the developed model in terms of potential validity and value in further analysis allows for scholastic license in evaluating the case studies.[81] As an untested model developed by the author, it is best to evaluate it against historical perspectives for evidence of validity. A plausibility probe analysis allows for a comparative study of the cases to validate or suppose that the model has value, in that it describes the potential impacts of external influences to the operational commander's risk decision. The model introduced in this study describes the balance a commander must strike between mission success and protection of the soldier over time. Where that balance exists is where the commander accepts risk to both the mission and the soldier, previously defined as prudent risk. This model proposes to describe the inadequacy of current doctrine in preparing and training commanders and staffs to adequately to balance risk to individuals and mission accomplishment with respect to strategic actors and their influence on the operational level of war. The following

---

[79] "Watching, Reading and Listening to the News," *Pew Research Center for the People and the Press*, n.d., http://www.people-press.org/2012/09/27/section-1-watching-reading-and-listening-to-the-news-3/ (accessed December 5, 2012).

[80] Alan Greenblatt, *Media Bias: Are the major sources of news trustworthy?*, The CQ Researcher Online Volume Number 14., Issue Number 36 (October 14, 2004), 855–875, http://library.cqpress.com/cqresearcher/cqresrre2004101500 (accessed January 12, 2013).

[81] Eckstein, *Regarding Politics*, 147.

case studies, sub-divided by phases in the operation will attempt to show a plausible causal relationship between the independent and dependent variables over time.

## CASE STUDIES

This research study will use the Iraq War (pre-war period through the exponential growth of the insurgency) as the case study for use with the author's unique methodology. As this methodology uses time as a factor in the shift of prudent risk, the case study will use time as the backbone for plausibility. In each time segment, the author will evaluate the products of the independent variable, casualty aversion, public support, consensus, and media position, as they relate to the dependent variable. Each phase will conclude with an aggregation pertaining to the plausibility of the model. Time Zero ($T_0$) is the phase of the Iraq War best characterized as the justification period where the Bush administration reevaluated the current policies regarding Iraq and decided on a course of action, coercive diplomacy. Time One ($T_1$) is the phase understood as the prelude for war when senior government leadership alerts the military, units prepare for combat, and commanders deploy for combat, focusing on offensive operations in Iraq beginning September 2002 through mid-March 2003. Time Two ($T_2$) is the period where major combat operations are ongoing beginning in mid-March 2003 through April 30, 2003. Time Three ($T_3$) is the instance when President George W. Bush gives his "Mission Accomplished" speech to the nation where he iterates that "the United States and our allies have prevailed…now our coalition is engaged in securing and reconstructing that country"[82] on May 1, 2003 through the end of July 2003. Time Four ($T_4$) is the period where commanders respond to the change in mission from offensive operations to stability operations beginning in August 2003 through December 2003.

---

[82] George W Bush, "President Declares End to Major Combat in Iraq," *CBS News*, n.d., http://www.cbsnews.com/8301-500257_162-551946.html (accessed November 22, 2012).

Finally, the case evaluation will conclude with an overall assessment as to the plausibility of the model advanced in this study.

Context for the War in Iraq – Time Zero (T0) – September 2001 to September 2002:

President George W. Bush's initial strategy for dealing with Iraq focused on the tightening of existing sanctions and using diplomacy to keep "Saddam in his box."[83] His justification at this time was the continued violation of United Nations resolutions and disruption of the no-fly-zone enforcement operations in place since 1991. After the attacks on September 11, 2001, the President took a fresh look at all threats globally.

In Iraq, he saw a state sponsor of terrorism, a sworn enemy of America, a hostile government that threatened its neighbors, a nation that violated international demands, a government that threatened and repressed its people, and a regime that pursued weapons of mass destruction.[84] Forced to look through the post-9/11 lens, the president saw Saddam Hussein as a significant threat and understood he could no longer ignore the problem.

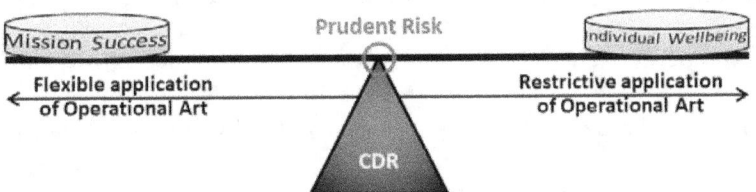

Figure 8: Time Zero ($T_0$).

*Source:* Created by the author.

---

[83] George W Bush, *Decision Points* (New York: Crown Publishers, 2010), 228.

[84] Ibid.

In ($T_0$) prudent risk balances between the mission and individual wellbeing. The mission during ($T_0$) actions consists of normal garrison activities (military/doctrinal training and professional military education). Individual wellbeing also consists of normal garrison activities best described as morale, welfare, and recreation opportunities afforded to soldiers and families. Army doctrine easily accounts for risk mitigation during this phase using the risk management process, "the process of identifying, assessing, and controlling risks arising from operational factors and making decisions that balance risk cost with mission benefits."[85] The process consists of five steps to control for risk, (1) identify hazards, (2) assess hazards to determine risks, (3) develop controls and make risk decisions, (4) implement controls, and (5) supervise and evaluate.[86] At issue, is that the doctrine does not effectively address those factors or hazards outside the control of the commander. Namely, the hazards the risk management process addresses are those that "have the potential to injure or kill friendly and civilian personnel, damage or destroy equipment, or otherwise impact mission effectiveness."[87] More specifically, the hazards the Composite Risk Management (CRM) process addressees are those that come "directly as the result of an enemy action or threat-based activity or as the result of other factors (hazard based), the CRM process *attempts* (emphasis added by author) to identify, assess, and control those factors that may adversely affect the capabilities of a military unit or organization."[88] This process works well for garrison activities and lower level tactical missions in this period but it may not work well when there is need to mitigate external sources (strategic actors) of hazard or risk.

---

[85] U.S. Department of the Army, *Army Doctrine Reference Publication 5-0*, 1–12.

[86] Ibid., 1–12.

[87] Ibid.

[88] U.S. Department of the Army, *Field Manual 5-19*, B–1.

Time One (T₁) – Prelude to war (Iraq) to posture for offensive operations September 2002 through mid-March 2003:

President Bush began with the use of "coercive diplomacy" that had a coalition and military component designed to influence Saddam to resign from government, give up weapons of mass destruction, end support of terrorism, and become a better neighbor.[89] September 7, 2002 marked the point at which the decision to move towards a war footing with Iraq emerged with backing from the United Nations. On November 8, the United Nations Security Council Resolution 1441 stated it was "*determined* to ensure full and immediate compliance by Iraq without conditions or restrictions with its obligations under Resolution 687 (1991) and other relevant resolutions and recalling that the resolutions of the Council constitute the governing standard of Iraqi compliance."[90] This resolution forced Saddam to comply with international demands, in particular to prove that he did not have weapons of mass destruction.

The international debates continued, as did Saddam's noncompliance, until President Bush decided that action was the course. On March 17, 2003, he addressed the nation and delivered the ultimatum to Saddam that he had forty-eight hours to leave Iraq or his "refusal to do so will result in military conflict."[91] The war began March 19, 2003 with the following mission objectives: "End the regime of Saddam Hussein... Eliminate Iraq's weapons of mass destruction...Capture or drive out terrorists...Collect intelligence on terrorist networks...Collect intelligence on Iraq's weapons of mass destruction activity...Secure Iraq's oil fields...Deliver humanitarian relief and end sanctions...Help Iraq achieve representative self-government and insure its territorial

---

[89] Bush, *Decision Points*, 230.

[90] UN Security Council, *United Nations Security Council Resolution 1441 (2002) Concerning Iraq*, S/RES/1441 (2002) (UN Security Council, 2002), 2.

[91] Bush, *Decision Points*, 253.

integrity."[92] Over the course of the next eight years, these objectives or manifestations of them drove the United States' war effort in Iraq.

For the operational commander, the prelude to war and deployment periods are the most important for his war efforts. In this timeframe, he will educate, train, equip, staff, and deploy his units in a fashion that ensures mission success. He will attempt to control the impacts strategic actors make on his units by balancing the risks to the mission and individual soldiers. This case study will look at how these actors affect the operational commander's preparations and readiness for war by analyzing casualty aversion, public support, Executive and Legislative Branch consensus, and mass media's position on the effort. The case study ends with the coalition postured for major combat operations in mid-March 2003.

Measuring casualty aversion in this period requires polling data for the citizen's viewpoint that the war is the correct or the incorrect option for the United States, or at this specific time, is going to war favored or opposed. In addition, measuring casualty aversion by the willingness of the American public to stay the course with military action in Iraq is as important. This study will analyze polling data that reflects the success or failure of the Bush administration's case for war to the American people. The aggregate of these measures indicates to what degree casualty aversion existed in the period analyzed.

Polling data from the period beginning September 2002 to mid-March 2003 evaluating the decision to go to war shows a consensus amongst the population sample that the decision to go to war was correct. For the time period, the responses that favor war never dip below 50 percent and those who opposed going to war never reached the 40 percent mark for the time

---

[92] Baker Spring, "Operation Iraqi Freedom: Military Objectives Met," *The Heritage Foundation - Leadership for America*, April 18, 2003, http://www.heritage.org/research/reports/2003/04/operation-iraqi-freedom-military-objectives-met (accessed November 27, 2012).

period. Graphic 1 in Appendix A shows the trends for both "favor" and "oppose" views. For this period, those favoring war shows a continued climb for supporting the war effort showing a general unwavering support for using military action to supplant the Saddam Hussein regime and adhere to the United Nations Security Council Resolution 1441 if he fails to comply. The "oppose" trend is generally downward for the period, indicating that those views are less prevalent as the nation geared up for the war. This period is typified by a majority of those polled viewing the prospect of war favorably.

The second measure for casualty aversion is the public's willingness to persevere, or in the prelude to war period, the success or failure of the administration's case that war is both a necessary and worthy endeavor. The Gallup Poll analysis ending March 15, 2003 asked adults "Do you think the Bush Administration has or has not made a convincing case about the need for the U.S. to take military action against Iraq?" The earliest poll, January 23-25, 2003 showed the case for war in Iraq split between those that believed the administration had made a viable case for war and those that did not believe the case presented with 49 percent and 48 percent respectively. Subsequently, those that believed the case for war made by the administration grew with each poll with the final two iterations garnering 56 percent and 57 percent for the war respectively (Graphic 6A, Appendix A).[93] The trend for those that believe the President successfully made a case for war turns upward, as more respondents agree that war is necessary and those that oppose that view decline. Graphic 2 in Appendix A shows the polling research for the study period for those that believed the war is worth the costs, or that it is necessary. Without a doubt, the case for war garnered majority support from the American people as well as their willingness to accept casualties from military personnel during this period.

---

[93] Jeffrey M. Jones, "Public Support for Iraq Invasion Inches Upward," *Gallup*, March 17, 2003, http://www.gallup.com/poll/7990/Public-Support-Iraq-Invasion-Inches-Upward.aspx (accessed December 4, 2012).

In 2005, Drs. Christopher Gelpi, Peter D. Feaver and Jason Reifler studied casualty sensitivity concerning the war in Iraq. They concluded, "Public support for the war reflects the mounting death toll combined with a perceived lack of measurable progress toward 'success.'"[94] Accurately measuring these indicators shall inform the study as to the amount of public support for the prelude to war. Similar to measuring casualty aversion, this section will use data derived from official sources for soldier combat death numbers and polling data that will measure the reasonable progress or confidence in a successful military operation.

For this particular time period where no combat deaths occurred, this study will look to polling data as to the expectation of casualties for the impending military operation. An ABC News Poll from March 5-9, 2003 asked 1,032 adults "Do you think there would or would not be a significant number of U.S. military casualties in a war with Iraq?" Respondents believed that there would be a significant number of casualties because of going to war with Iraq, 65 percent and 62 percent for February and March polling respectively.[95] Additionally, a CBS News Poll asked 868 adults through March 26-27, 2003 "do you think removing Saddam Hussein from power is worth the potential loss of American life and the other costs of attacking Iraq, or not" with respondents believing overwhelmingly that it was worth the costs.[96] These polls are indicative of many other polls conducted during the preparation for war period. The majority of respondents believed that the costs would be worth the efforts to rid Iraq of Saddam Hussein (Graphic 6B, Appendix A) with one notable exception in late October, 2002.[97] Clearly, the

---

[94] Gelpi, Feaver, and Reifler, "Success Matters," 9.

[95] PollingReport.com, "Iraq," *PollingReport.com*, n.d., 18, http://www.pollingreport.com/iraq.htm (accessed December 4, 2012).

[96] Ibid., 17.

[97] Ibid.

expectation of the American people is that there will be a cost in lives lost with military action in Iraq and that cost in lives is worth it and necessary.

Public support for the war effort revolved around the prospects for success. Underpinning many early views on the likelihood for victory was the Persian Gulf War fought in 1991. Many Americans looked to that experience to formulate their opinion on the chances the military has for success and these optimistic views reflected in the polling data. A Gallup Poll conducted on March 17, 2003 "after President Bush's ultimatum to Saddam, found 79 percent of Americans saying the United States would be successful in its goal of removing him from power. Only 13 percent believe it will be unsuccessful."[98] Americans readily supported America's march to war with Iraq and believed it would be successful.

The evidence for Executive and Legislative Branch consensus is demonstrated in House Joint Resolution 114 authorizing the use of military force against Iraq. This Resolution passed the House on October 10, 2002 with 296 votes in favor and 133 votes against its enactment. It passed the Senate on October 11, 2002 with 77 affirmative votes and 23 negative votes.[99] This resolution states "The President is authorized to use the Armed Forces of the United States as he determines to be necessary and appropriate in order to—(1) defend the national security of the United States against the continuing threat posed by Iraq; and (2) enforce all relevant United Nations Security Council resolutions regarding Iraq."[100] Clearly, both chambers of the Legislative Branch concur

---

[98] Frank Newport, David W. Moore, and Jeffrey M. Jones, "Special Release: American Opinion on the War," *Gallup*, March 21, 2003, http://www.gallup.com/poll/8068/Special-Release-American-Opinion-War.aspx (accessed December 5, 2012).

[99] Project Vote Smart, "'Iraq' 2002 National Key Votes," *Project Vote Smart*, n.d., https://votesmart.org/bills/NA/2002/?state=NA&category=&year=2002&search=iraq#.UL6fMIZ CN8H (accessed December 5, 2012).

[100] House Committee on Committee on International Relations, *Authorization For Use of Military Force Against Iraq Resolution of 2002*, 107th Cong., 2d sess., 2002, H. Rep. 721, 4.

with the necessity to use military force to remove Saddam Hussein from power in Iraq. With this resolution passing, strong consensus for war existed between the Executive and Legislative Branches.

The influence of mass media during this period was a measure for exposure the American public receives over the course of a given month. The measure is in minutes devoted by news affiliates to combat in Iraq and general stories pertaining to Iraq. Graphic 5 in Appendix A displays the amount of minutes the major affiliates devoted to stories about combat in Iraq and the total number of minutes devoted to stories about Iraq. For this period, the American people's exposure was limited early as the debate for war in Iraq was just starting. Towards the end of the period, the debate of whether or not to go to war against Iraq began to spike with more than 355 minutes of exposure to stories about Iraq. Clearly, the American media bombarded the public with stories about Iraq.

For ($T_1$), the evidence suggests that casualty aversion was low, public support for military operations was high, both the Executive and Legislative Branches were in consensus with regards to military operations, and the mass media was supportive of going to war. The strategic actors supported the impending combat with Iraq and in supporting the war, applied pressure on mission success. In placing their combined weight on mission success, the strategic actors are willing to accept risk to the individual service member's wellbeing (Figure 9).

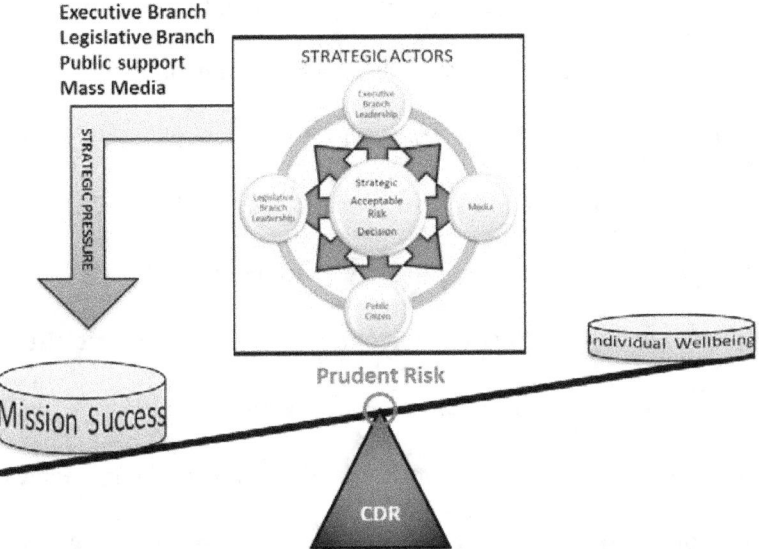

**T₁ (September 2002 through mid-March 2003) = Prelude to war (Iraq) to posture for offensive operations – risk is out of balance and individual wellbeing is seconded to achieving objectives. Casualty aversion is low, public support is strong, Executive and Legislative consensus is solid, and the mass media is in favor of military operations**

Figure 9: Time One (T₁).

*Source:* Created by the author.

This added weight throws the commander's risk equation out of balance and requires him to reevaluate the plan and how he will employ the elements of operational art to link the upcoming tactical actions to the strategic objectives outlined in his orders. Where and how he accepts this risk is entirely at his discretion. He is time constrained and can only rely on his experience, limited risk management training, knowledge, and the limited doctrinal exposure he has to assessing, mitigating, and controlling for risk before combat operations begin in (T₂). The evidence clearly shows plausibility for the model in this period. This period and perhaps (T₂) are the only ones, according to the proposed model, that the doctrine may substantially help the commander due to the major combat related nature of the periods.

Time Two ($T_2$) – Fight the ground war mid-March through April 30, 2003:

At the outset of actual combat operations in Iraq, commanders made decisions that affected both the mission and wellbeing of soldiers. They must ultimately succeed in their military objective, so his default priorities focus to that end. For the operational commander, combat operations naturally flow from the preparation for combat ($T_1$) period. The time for education, training, equipping, staffing, and deploying is over and his units are prepared to engage the enemy in lethal combat. Most units seek to secure physical objectives with the remainder aiding them in that effort. Speed and audacity permeate the language of orders along with seizing and retaining initiative. Commanders abhor caution and timidity in their subordinate leaders and will unflinchingly support those commanders that exhibit aggression and decisiveness. With his risk equation out of balance towards mission accomplishment, the commander will attempt to control the impacts strategic actors make on his units by trying to re-balance the risk equation. Similar to ($T_1$), the strategic actors start with broad-based support for combat operations. Strategic actors are expected to generate support for the war giving the operational commander flexibility in his application of operational art. This case will look at how these actors affect the operational commander's ability to prosecute the ground combat phase of the war by analyzing casualty aversion, public support, Executive and Legislative Branch consensus, and mass media's position on the effort. The case will end with a conclusion for this time period.

As with ($T_1$), measuring casualty aversion in this period requires polling data for the citizen's viewpoint that the war is the correct or the incorrect option for the United States and that it is favored or opposed. In addition, it is important to measure casualty aversion by the willingness of the American public to stay the course as casualties and costs mount with military action in Iraq. For this period, analysis of polling data that reflects the weight the public places on

46

the worthiness of the war effort was conducted. The aggregate of these measures indicates to what degree casualty aversion existed in the period analyzed.

Polling data from the period beginning mid-March 2003 through the end of April 2003 covering the correctness of the decision to go to war shows a consensus amongst the population sample that the decision to go to war was correct. For this time period, the "favor" responses climb to a peak of 75 percent and those opposed to going to war sank to the low of 21 percent in the time period. Graphic 1 in Appendix A shows the trends for both "favor" and "oppose" views. For this period, those favoring war shows a continued climb for supporting the war effort for the two-month segment showing a sharp building of support for combat operations to supplant the Saddam Hussein regime. The "oppose" trend remains generally downward for the period, indicating that those views are less prevalent. Clearly, this period shows the large majority of Americans supporting the ongoing combat operations in Iraq.

The second measure for casualty aversion was the public's view that the effort was worth the costs. Several polls in this time period asked respondents about the costs of war in terms of casualties and other costs. A continuing poll from ABC News/Washington Post asked registered voters "Again thinking about the goals versus the costs of the war, so far in your opinion has there been an acceptable or unacceptable number of U.S. military casualties in Iraq?"[101] In three iterations of this poll during ($T_2$), respondents answered that the casualties were acceptable (58 percent, 62 percent, and 66 percent) (Graphic 6C, Appendix A). As expected, the numbers of Americans who believed the costs in casualties was not worth the risk declined. Graphic 2 in Appendix A, shows that there was consensus amongst the American populace that the costs were worthy of the effort. Without a doubt, the case for war garnered majority support from the American people as well as their willingness to accept casualties during this period.

---

[101] PollingReport.com, "Polling Report," 11.

Measuring the public's support for war hinges on two measures, the mounting death toll of service members and the perceived lack of progress towards success. This section will use data derived from official sources for soldier combat death numbers and polling data that will be used to measure the reasonable progress or confidence in a successful military operation.

For this particular period, combat related deaths were relatively low. In March 2003, fifty United States military service members died due to combat related actions and another 58 died in April totaling 108 U.S. service member combat deaths.[102] At the outbreak of major combat operations in March 2003, the United States military attacked Iraq with approximately 150,000 personnel.[103] Comparatively, the first named major combat operation in Vietnam, Operation Starlight fought over a period of two days the United States Marine Corps suffered forty-five combat related deaths out of the 5,500 marines who participated.[104] A Time/CNN Poll conducted by Harris Interactive asked 1,001 adults nationwide "in your view, is the war against Iraq worth the toll it has taken in American lives and other kinds of costs, or isn't the war worth these costs?"[105] The majority of the respondents believed that the war was worth the costs in American lives (59 percent). Additionally, the ABC News/Washington Post Poll speaks to the American views that the numbers of combat deaths in Iraq for the March to April 2003 period was in fact acceptable to oust Saddam Hussein. Looking solely at combat related deaths for the first two months of fighting in Iraq, the numbers of casualties appears to be within an acceptable threshold for the American public.

---

[102] "iCasualties | Operation Iraqi Freedom | Iraq," *Iraq Coalition Casualty Count*, n.d., http://www.icasualties.org/Iraq/index.aspx (accessed January 12, 2013).

[103] Bush, *Decision Points*, 250.

[104] Jack Shulimson, *U.S. Marines in Vietnam: the Landing and the Buildup, 1965* (Nashville, Tenn.: Battery Press, 1996), 65–83.

[105] PollingReport.com, "Polling Report," 14.

Public support for the war effort also revolved around the prospects for success. In order to measure success in the war effort, polling data for this period asked Americans their feelings on whether the coalition is winning or losing. Graphic 3 in Appendix A shows the accumulation of polling data asking Americans whether they believe the U.S. is winning or losing the war in Iraq. Clearly, in the period containing the start of combat operations through the end of April 2003, Americans strongly believed that the U.S. was winning the war with Iraq. In fact, the end of April marks the peak for these beliefs. Clearly, Americans readily supported the war with Iraq.

The evidence for Executive and Legislative Branch consensus came from legislation that occurred during the period. On April 3, 2003, Congress passed HR 1559, the Emergency Wartime Supplemental Appropriations Act with a vote reflecting overwhelming support by 414 representatives to twelve dissenters in the House of Representatives and no members of the Senate dissenting. This law enacted by the President on April 19 made immediately available $62 billion for military operations in Iraq.[106] Clearly, both chambers of the Legislative Branch concurred with the necessity to support the ongoing war with Iraq. With this Public Law's adoption, very strong consensus for supporting the war existed between the Executive and Legislative Branches.

For time period two, mass media devoted the most minutes to both stories of combat in Iraq and overall stories pertaining to Iraq for the entirety of this study. Understandably, American service members were conducting major combat operations and the military leadership strongly supported the embedding of media in their formations. Military leaders knew the importance of telling their story to the American people and the embed program was the best means to do so. Because of this program, mass media devoted 869 minutes of coverage to combat actions in Iraq

---

[106] Project Vote Smart, "'Iraq' 2003 National Key Votes," *Project Vote Smart*, n.d., https://votesmart.org/bills/NA/2003/?state=NA&category=&year=2003&search=iraq#.UL6hK4Z CN8E (accessed December 5, 2012).

for the period. Additionally, the mass media devoted an additional 1,378 minutes to general stories about Iraq (Graphic 5, Appendix A). A Media Monitor study finished in August 2003 found that the "combined war related opinion on the three broadcast networks was evenly balanced," airing stories in support and opposition to the war effort.[107] Clearly, the American media increased the exposure of the war effort to the American people, allowing them to formulate their own personal feelings of support or opposition for the war effort.

For ($T_2$), the evidence suggests that casualty aversion remains low, public support for military operations remains high, both the Executive and Legislative Branches are in consensus concerning military operations, and the mass media is supportive of the war. The strategic actors support ongoing combat in Iraq. By so heavily supporting the war, the pressure these actors exert through the products of casualty aversion, public support, consensus, and positive media coverage placed continued weight on accomplishing the mission with less concern for the individual soldier's wellbeing. With this added weight and support for combat operations, the commander can now balance his risk equation through very flexible application of operational art (Figure 10).

---

[107] S. Robert Lichter and Linda S. Lichter, "Media Monitor: The Media Go to War TV News Coverage of the War in Iraq," *CMPA: Center for Media and Public Affairs*, August 2003, 5–6, http://www.cmpa.com/files/media_monitor/03novdec.pdf (accessed January 16, 2013).

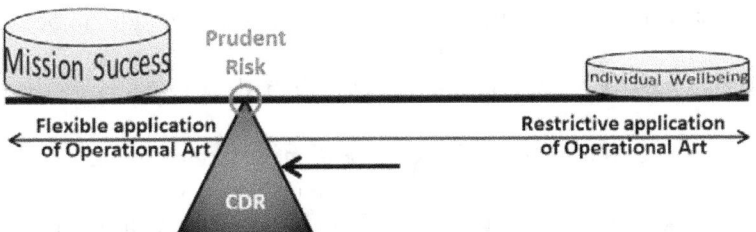

T₂ (mid-March through April 30, 2003) = Fight the ground war (KINETIC) – Offensive operations and the commander responds to order; risk is re-balanced with more options available and flexibility in applying operational art with more willingness to accept casualties, public support for offensive operations, consensus within the Executive and Legislative Branches, and mass media is support of the effort. *Examples of military actions: Thunder Runs in Baghdad, airborne operations in Northern Iraq, deep attacks with aviation assets unsupported by ground forces, and POWs*

Figure 10: Time Two (T₂).

*Source:* Created by the author.

He has more options available to him with fewer exerted restrictions, whether they are minimizing casualties or careful execution of the mission directed through the chain of command. Speed, aggression, flexibility, and initiative are all available to the commander to exploit success on the battlefield. He need not be overly cautious in how he deploys his forces and conducts combat operations. In an interview by Cami McCormick on March 27, 2003, General Tommy Franks affirmed this belief when he answered, "I think one of the bits of evidence of a good plan is the flexibility to respond to what we find. We know this. We know that the most capable armed forces in the world are a part of this coalition. And if you take the most capable forces in the world you equip them with the right kind of equipment and you put them in motion, with a very flexible plan that the outcome is not in doubt."[108] So long as he is successful, the strategic actors allow for casualties as part of warfare. Using the operations process, the commander will employ

---

[108] Tommy Franks, "General Tommy Franks," Radio, March 27, 2003, http://www.freerepublic.com/focus/f-news/878280/posts (accessed January 12, 2012).

the elements of operational art to link the tactical actions to the strategic objectives outlined in his order, which will rebalance his risk equation. As with $(T_1)$, doctrine does a reasonable job at preparing the commander and his staff to identify prudent risk in this time period. Where and how he uses that doctrine to accept this risk is entirely at his discretion with the full support of the strategic actors. The evidence presented for this time period lends to the plausibility of the model proposed in this paper.

Time Three $(T_3)$ – Mission Accomplished and transition from Offensive to Stability Operations early May 2003 through July 2003:

On May 1 2003, President Bush landed aboard the aircraft carrier USS *Abraham Lincoln*. His intention was to send a message to the American people and coalition partners that the war in Iraq is starting a new phase, not that the mission was accomplished. With the fall of Baghdad, the Saddam regime was no longer in control of Iraq and all efforts should now focus on "helping the Iraqis develop a democracy that could govern itself, sustain itself, defend itself, and serve as an ally in the war on terror."[109] In American military doctrine, this transition describes the intended shift from major combat operations to stability operations, also known as Phase IV operations.[110] Several books, editorials, testimonies, and commentaries criticizing the preparedness of the coalition to conduct this phase of operation exist; this study will not devolve into that argument as it is outside the scope of the study. Instead, the study of this time period will focus on the immediate aftermath of President Bush's speech aboard the Lincoln to the end of July 2003.

For the operational commander, the transition from major combat operations to stability operations requires an appreciation for the joint concept of termination. As a part of operational design, termination requires the operational commander to understand and account for "a wide

---

[109] Bush, *Decision Points*, 257.

[110] U.S. Joint Chiefs of Staff, *Joint Publication 3-0*, GL–16.

variety of operational tasks that the joint force may need to accomplish, to include disengagement, force protection, transition to post-conflict operations, reconstitution, and redeployment."[111] The concept of termination typifies this phase of the overall war in Iraq. Perhaps unintentionally, President Bush set in motion this phase of the operation where the operational commander's risk equation is again out of balance. The operational commander began to focus on post-offensive operations, preserving the force, war termination efforts, and military draw down in the war zone. This case will look at how these actors affect the operational commander's termination of offensive operations and the transition to stability operations for war by analyzing casualty aversion, public support, Executive and Legislative Branch consensus, and mass media's position on the effort. The case will end with a conclusion for this time period.

As Graphic 1 in Appendix A depicts, polling data from May 1 2003 through July 2003 shows a steady decline in the percentage of those Americans that support the war effort. Still, the majority of the polled population still supports the effort. For the time period, the "favor" responses never dipped below 60 percent and those opposed to going to war views never rose to the 40 percent mark for the period. For this period, those supporting the war showed a steady decline for continued war, indicating a general uneasiness of the population to the reasons for continuing the war. Clearly, there was a growing trepidation in the public sector for continuation of the war effort.

The willingness of the American people to persevere in the efforts against Iraq is the second measure of casualty aversion. This period will examine whether the American public still saw the effort as worth the continued costs. Graphic 2 in Appendix A examines the views of Americans as to the costs associated with the war effort. Indicative for the period is a decline in

---

[111] U.S. Joint Chiefs of Staff, *Joint Operation Planning*, Joint Publication 5-0 (Washington, D.C.: U.S. Joint Chiefs of Staff, 2011), III–19.

those respondents that viewed the continued war effort as worth the costs. From a peak of 70 percent at the end of $(T_2)$ to just above 50 percent at the end of $(T_3)$ a dramatic shift occurs in the willingness of the public to see the worthiness of the war effort. Logically, it follows that there was a genuine increase in those Americans that believed the war effort was no longer worth the blood and treasure poured into Iraq. Graphic 2 of Appendix A depicts this swing in support rather well. Undoubtedly, the American people were losing their taste for war and their willingness to accept casualties associated with a mission articulated as already accomplished. Perhaps, in the minds of Americans, the wellbeing of soldiers was starting to weigh more heavily.

Looking to public support for the war, this study will examine the mounting death toll in combination with the perceived amount of progress the coalition is achieving in the war effort. Accurately measuring these indicators shall inform the study as to the amount of public support for the continuation of the war in Iraq. This section will use data derived from official sources for soldier combat death numbers and polling data that will measure the reasonable progress or confidence in a successful military operation.

In determining whether Americans viewed the additional 54 combat related deaths in Iraq for the period as acceptable, a review of polling data will provide insight. A poll conducted in July 2003 by CNN, USA Today, and Gallup asked 1,005 adults nationwide, "thinking about how the U.S. should deal with the situation in Iraq in the future, which would you prefer -- to continue to have a significant number of U.S. troops in Iraq for as long as needed regardless of how many U.S. military service people are killed, to withdraw all U.S. troops from Iraq if the number of U.S. military service people who are killed becomes too high, or to withdraw all U.S. troops from Iraq now?"[112] The responses were 37 percent committed to staying as long as needed, 33 percent believed we should withdraw if too many are killed, and 26 percent believed we should withdraw

---

[112] PollingReport.com, "Polling Report," 12.

immediately with 4 percent unsure about how they felt. The mounting casualties after the declared end to major combat operations appears to be taking a toll on the American people, but not to a degree that support for the war effort is on the verge of collapse from casualties alone.

The perceived success, or not, of operations following the end of major combat operations will provide the second critical measure as to whether public support for the war effort continues in this period. Although remaining above the 50 percent threshold for positive views on the nature of the operation as successful, no three-month span of time studied showed a more precipitous drop than during ($T_3$). Graphic 3 in Appendix A depicts this drop from 73 percent in May 2003 to just 53 percent in July 2003. Clearly, in this period after the completion of major combat operations and transition to stability operations, Americans were showing less confidence in whether the U.S. was winning the war with Iraq.

The evidence for Executive and Legislative Branch consensus in this period is still strong. During the period, Congress proposed four pieces of legislation that covered the war effort in Iraq in general. On May 22, 2003, Congress passed The Defense Department Fiscal Year 2004 Authorization Bill, with a vote reflecting substantial support by 361 representatives and 98 senators.[113] This law made available almost $400 billion for military operations in the next fiscal year. The three other pieces of legislation focused on terrorism information awareness, foreign operations appropriations for nations supportive of efforts in Iraq, and Veteran's Affairs.[114] Each of these received vast majority support in both the House of Representatives and the Senate, evidence that both chambers of the Legislative Branch concurred with the necessity to support the ongoing war with Iraq. For this period, there is strong evidence that consensus for continued

---

[113] Project Vote Smart, "'Iraq' 2003 Key Votes."

[114] Ibid.

support of the war exists between the Executive and Legislative Branches, focused not on combat operations but on rebuilding a broken nation.

For period three, mass media devoted less minutes to both stories of combat in Iraq and overall stories pertaining to Iraq than in the previous period. Graphic 5 in Appendix A shows the amount of minutes devoted to combat and Iraq in general it dropped precipitously in May 2003 to 39 minutes and 192 minutes respectively. Many of these stories in May were devoted to the successful completion of combat operations for the war, specifically linked to President Bush's speech. However, as time passed from May to July, the amount of minutes spent on combat and Iraq began to increase with a total of 150 minutes devoted to stories of combat and 409 minutes pertaining to Iraq. In conjunction with the increase in minutes, so too did the negative stories related to both the President and his war time policies with "evaluations directed toward President Bush ran over two-to-one negative (68 percent negative vs. 32 percent positive)" and "the administration's policies received even worse press than the president and his appointees...three out every four of these evaluations were critical (77 percent negative)."[115] Coupled with more minutes devoted and an increasingly negative tone to the coverage, the impact of the media sharply moved away from the glowing support provided in the previous time periods. Clearly, the American media greatly increased the negative exposure of those policies surrounding the war effort, perhaps influencing the increased levels of casualty aversion and lessening of public support for the war effort.

For ($T_3$), the evidence suggests that casualty aversion is steadily increasing but not critically, public support for military operations is dropping, both the Executive and Legislative

---

[115] S. Robert Lichter and Linda S. Lichter, "Media Monitor: George Bush's Postwar Blues TV News Coverage of President Bush Since the Iraq War," *CMPA: Center for Media and Public Affairs*, December 2003, 4–6, http://www.cmpa.com/files/media_monitor/03novdec.pdf (accessed January 16, 2013).

Branches remain in consensus with regards to military operations, and the mass media is turning away support for the ongoing war effort. With the declared end to major combat operations, the strategic actors are beginning to support the war effort less than previous periods. As the support for the mission shifts away, it begins to place more influence on the wellbeing of the soldiers deployed in the combat zone. Additionally, according to Lieutenant General Ricardo S. Sanchez, General Tommy Franks was planning for a major force reduction in Iraq to offset American discontent from a prolonged war.[116]

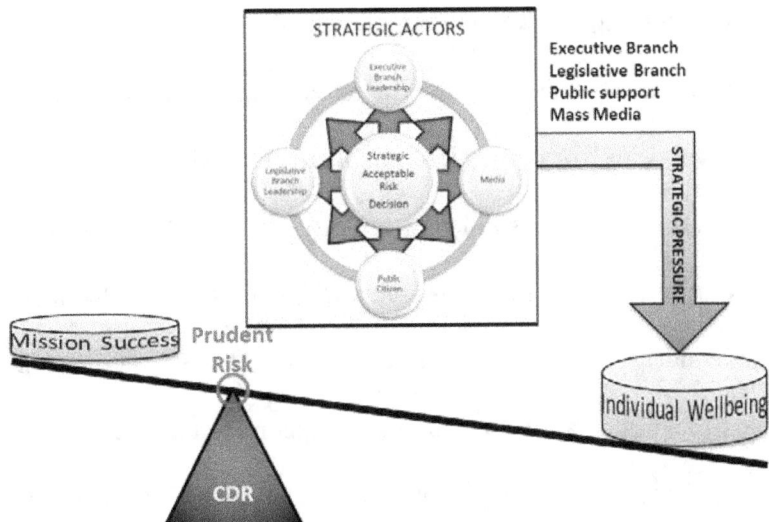

$T_3$ (May 1, 2003 through July 2003) = Mission accomplished and transition from offensive to stability operations (mission order received - NONKINETIC) – risk is placed out of balance with post-offensive operations focused on preserving the force, war termination efforts, and military draw down in war zone. *Examples of military actions: 101st ABN early COIN functions in Mosul, Sunni triangle violence, religious attacks and division, and reduction in forces*

Figure 15: Time Three ($T_3$).

*Source:* Created by the author.

---

[116] Ricardo S. Sanchez, *Wiser in Battle: A Soldier's Story* (New York, NY: HarperCollins, 2008), 168.

Perhaps the speech that started this period provides a lens into why the shift in support changed. In President Bush's speech aboard the USS *Abraham Lincoln* on May 1 2003, he stated that "In the Battle of Iraq, the United States and our allies have prevailed…now our coalition is engaged in securing and reconstructing that country…the tyrant has fallen, and Iraq is free…we are helping to rebuild Iraq…stand with the new leaders of Iraq as they establish a government of, by, and for the Iraqi people. The transition from dictatorship to democracy will take time, but it is worth every effort. Our coalition will stay until our work is done. And then we will leave — and we will leave behind a free Iraq."[117] The public, as well as the congressional representatives may construe these statements as a policy shift from major combat operations to a policy of stability operations that looks very similar to operations conducted in the Balkans. Those operations resulted in eight U.S. service members killed, much different from the 48 service members killed in this post-major combat period. In Iraq, this added weight onto the wellbeing of individuals imbalances the commander's risk equation and requires him to reevaluate the plan and how he will employ the elements of operational art to link the upcoming tactical actions to the new strategic objectives outlined in his order. Again, doctrine informs him that where and how he accepts this risk is entirely his discretion. However, he is further constrained by lessening support for combat operations, remains time constrained and can only rely on his experience, limited risk management training, knowledge, and the limited doctrinal exposure to assess, mitigate, and control for risk in preparation for stability operations. The commander, caught between his own evaluation of risk and the influence exerted from the strategic actors must now attempt to change course. He is still suffering casualties at the hands of the enemy and now feels pressure to limit those casualties as the transition to stability operations begin, including a planned troop reduction. There is no clean break between combat operations and stability operations, so he must attempt

---

[117] Bush, "President Declares End to Major Combat in Iraq."

the transition carefully so that he does not incur additional external pressures. Current doctrine for risk management does little in preparing the commander and his staff for this period, which provides added evidence as to the plausibility of the proposed model.

Time Four ($T_4$) – Stability Operations to the transfer of sovereignty August 2003 through June 2004:

By the end of July, the Coalition Provisional Authority (CPA) recognized internationally, instituted three major decisions that would profoundly influence operational commanders in Iraq for years to come.[118] Two of these decisions took place almost immediately after Ambassador L. Paul Bremer arrived in Iraq. First, he announced the purge of "some 30,000 senior Ba'ath party members from public employment," effectively removing from office those Iraqis that understood the inner workings of the nation's economy, infrastructure, and governing bodies.[119] The second decision was the disbanding of the Iraqi army, which effectively created an estimated 230,000 unemployed military aged males from the commissioned and non-commissioned ranks; many argue this action birthed the impending insurgency. The third decision was the creation of the Governing Council. On July 13, 2003, a 25-person Iraqi Governing Council met with an eventual goal of returning sovereignty to Iraq at the soonest opportunity. Their first order of business was to select a president.[120] Unable to come to consensus on a candidate, the council "chose instead to have a nine-man presidency that would rotate monthly."[121] As the operational commanders wrestled with decisions about force size, his transition from major combat operations to stability

---

[118] James Dobbins et al., *Occupying Iraq: a History of the Coalition Provisional Authority* (Santa Monica, CA: RAND Corp, 2009). An extensive history for the origins and functions of the CPA for the Iraq War.

[119] Ibid., 28.

[120] Ibid., 46.

[121] Ibid.

operations, and widespread security lapses, the CPA created an additional layer of complexity for him to address as he attempts to rebalance his risk equation.

In a similar manner as ($T_2$), the commander was in an unbalanced position regarding risk. He still must meet his strategic objectives while keeping in mind the wellbeing of individuals. As the pressure mounts on his scale, he must apply operational art in a manner that returns balance to the risk equation. For this period, the pressure exerted was skewed toward individual wellbeing. Strategic actors start with broad-based support for the complete transition to stability operations and timely return of America's service members. As described by the model, strategic actors will begin replacing support for the war effort with concern for the wellbeing of service members, reducing the flexibility and options available to the operational commander. As the reduction in options takes effect, the operational commander finds his options and flexibility in applying operational art limited. This case will look at how these actors affected the operational commander's ability to prosecute the stability operations phase of the war by analyzing casualty aversion, public support, Executive and Legislative Branch consensus, and mass media's position on the effort. The case will end with a conclusion for this period.

Polling data from the period beginning August 2003 through June 2004 covering the correctness of the decision to go to war shows a continued decline in the percentage of those Americans that support the war effort (Graphic 1, Appendix A). There are three aberrations to this trend. The first is in September 2003 where the trend reverses, more than likely attributed to the second anniversary of the attacks on America.[122] The second reversal coincides with the capture of Saddam Hussein in December 2003. The third peak during the period roughly coincides with the graphic and brutal images of the four U.S. security contractors killed in

---

[122] For the entirety of the study frame (September 2002 through April 2006), every September shows a peak in regards to support for the war with Iraq.

Fallujah in March 2004. Still, during this period the majority of the polled population supported the effort in Iraq. For most the time period, the "favor" responses stay well below 60 percent and those opposed to going to war views hovered close to the 40 percent mark. For this period, those supporting the war show a steady decline for continued war, indicating a general weariness for continuing the war. The "oppose" trend is generally upward for the period, indicating a growing apprehension for continuing war in Iraq. Evidently, there was mounting anxiety in the public sector for continuation of the war effort.

The second measure for casualty aversion is the public's view that the effort was worth the costs to rid the world of the Saddam Hussein regime. Several polls in this time period asked respondents about the costs of war in terms of casualties and other costs. Continuing with a poll from the previous two periods, an ABC News/Washington Post Poll asked registered voters "Again thinking about the goals versus the costs of the war, so far in your opinion has there been an acceptable or unacceptable number of U.S. military casualties in Iraq?"[123] Continuing from ($T_3$), Graphic 6C in Appendix A shows the public's concern for casualties and costs is growing steadily, crossing the 50 percent mark in July 2003 and never again rising above that majority threshold. The aggregate polling data (Graphic 2 in Appendix A) for the period shows more fluctuation in those Americans weighing the costs of the war. Ironically, the period's average return for those that still believe the costs are worth the effort was 52 percent. More importantly, this period reflects the downward trend through the 50 percent threshold where those that continue to believe the costs are worth the effort increasingly become the minority. Looking at the two measures for casualty aversion, there was growing concern for the mounting casualties and costs for the war.

---

[123] PollingReport.com, "Polling Report," 11.

Looking to public support for the war, this study will examine the mounting death toll in combination with the perceived amount of progress the coalition is achieving in the war effort. Accurately measuring these indicators shall inform the study as to the amount of public support for the continuation of the war in Iraq. This section will use data derived from official sources for soldier combat death numbers and polling data that will measure the reasonable progress or confidence in a successful military operation.

For this period, combat related deaths continued to mount at an average of just under 43 service members killed each month. In April 2004, the greatest number of service member combat related deaths in the war to date occurred. It also marked the highest monthly total for the span of aggregated data for this study, 126 service members were killed due to combat related incidents. In determining whether Americans viewed the numbers of deaths in Iraq for the period as acceptable, the study turns to existing polling data. A CBS News/New York Times Poll compiled through July 25, 2006 asked "Do you think the result of the war with Iraq was worth the loss of American life and other costs of attacking Iraq, or not?"[124] Graphic 6D in Appendix A shows the results of the poll. In this period, Americans clearly felt that the effort in Iraq is no longer worthy of the sacrifice in deaths to service members. Throughout the period, those that believe continued casualties are worth the effort declines from 46 percent to a low of 32 percent at the end of the period. Looking solely at combat related deaths for this period, the numbers of casualties appears to detract support from the war effort. The American people were withdrawing their support at an increasing rate; the majority believed the effort is not worth American lives.

The second measure of public support is the prospect for success in the war effort. The aggregation of polling data related to success or failure appears in Graphic 3, Appendix A. Highlighting the period are two segments of decline in the perceived prospects for success and a

---

[124] Ibid., 10.

single segment that shows a majority view that the war will result in success. The first segment shows a continuing decline from the previous case period presenting a pessimistic view for the outcome of the war. This period transitions to the only optimistic segment of time prompted by the capture of Saddam Hussein in December 2003 and ending with the vicious killing of the U.S. security contractors in Fallujah. The next segment begins a sharply pessimistic view by the American people through the end of the case period. For the preponderance of ($T_4$), Americans retain a largely pessimistic outlook for the war effort in Iraq. Clearly, in this case period the American people no longer thought a successful outcome in Iraq was likely and were steadily pulling support for continued operations in Iraq.

Examining the nature of the legislation will give a better understanding of the degree of consensus between the Executive and Legislative branches. During the period, Congress proposed several pieces of legislation spanning the war effort in Iraq.[125] Three bills focused on appropriations relating to the ongoing war effort in Iraq (including the war in Afghanistan). Two bills focused directly on service member support and appreciation. Two House resolutions spoke directly to the Iraqi people. Interestingly, most of this legislation passed with greater than a simple majority. In terms of legislation that focused on the individual service member, veterans, families, and protective equipment for service members, Congress was in clear consensus with the Executive Branch. They were continuing support for the war effort but from the standpoint of supporting the service members and not necessarily the policies of the President. The growing opposition began to voice publicly its opposition to President Bush's policies towards Iraq. Candidate Howard Dean provides an example of the growing opposition when he stated in an

---

[125] Project Vote Smart, "'Iraq' 2003 Key Votes"; Project Vote Smart, "'Iraq' 2004 National Key Votes," Project Vote Smart, n.d., https://votesmart.org/bills/NA/2004/?state=NA&category=&year=2003&search=iraq#.UL6hK4Z CN8E (accessed December 5, 2012).

Iowa Democratic Primary during this case period that he "did not support the policy but I always support the troops" when asked about Iraq.[126] Congress's support for legislation geared towards the individual service member was steadily growing and their support for war policies was in steady decline, demonstrating a separation in the consensus between the Executive and Legislative Branches.

Iraq remained the most televised story for 2003 and 2004, garnering approximately 30 percent of all stories ran in 2003 and 25 percent in 2004.[127] For ($T_4$), mass media devoted the preponderance of news airtime to both stories of combat in Iraq and overall stories pertaining to Iraq, 1,120 minutes and 3,004 minutes respectively (Graphic 5, Appendix A).[128] The major stories garnering this attention were the continued search and eventual capture of Saddam Hussein, a David Kay interview that refuted the existence of Iraqi Weapons of Mass Destruction, the dramatic and inhuman video of the U.S. security contractor killings in Fallujah, the revelation of the Abu Ghraib prisoner abuses, and the transfer of sovereignty to the Iraqi government. Perhaps only two of these major storylines are viewable in a positive light for the war effort and policies. The eventual capture of Saddam Hussein and the transfer of sovereignty from the coalition occupation forces to the Iraqi government. The continued questioning of the evidence for the war and the policies keeping service members in Iraq demonstrated the negative connotation the mass

---

[126] "Democratic Presidential Candidate's Debate," *CNN*, January 4, 2004, http://transcripts.cnn.com/TRANSCRIPTS/0401/04/se.01.html (accessed January 18, 2013).

[127] S. Robert Lichter and Linda S. Lichter, "Media Monitor: 2003 Year in Review," CMPA: Center for Media and Public Affairs, February 2004, 1–2, http://www.cmpa.com/files/media_monitor/04janfeb.pdf (accessed January 16, 2013); S. Robert Lichter and Linda S. Lichter, "Media Monitor: 2004 Year in Review," CMPA: Center for Media and Public Affairs, February 2005, 1–2, http://www.cmpa.com/files/media_monitor/05janfeb.pdf (accessed January 16, 2013).

[128] Andrew Tyndall, "Tyndall Report monthly breakdown for yearly stories", January 11, 2013.

media took concerning Iraq. Similar to ($T_3$), the increasing amount of minutes devoted, the increasingly negative tone to the coverage, and the impact of mass media's continued pessimistic coverage of the war in Iraq greatly increased the negative exposure of those policies surrounding the war effort, perhaps influencing the increased levels of casualty aversion and lessening of public support for the war effort.

For ($T_4$), the evidence suggests that casualty aversion continues to increase from ($T_3$) and is now the majority position with Americans, public support for military operations continues dropping so that the majority is now opposed to the war effort, both the Executive and Legislative Branches are showing strains in consensus with regards to the policies surrounding military operations in Iraq, and the mass media is turning very critical for the ongoing war effort. With the declared end to major combat operations, the strategic actors have clearly switched support for the mission to support for service members in this period. The increased pressure to the individual wellbeing of service members clearly limits the options the operational commander has available to respond to mission requirements and successfully completing his strategic objectives. He is no longer free to accept larger amounts of risk with soldier wellbeing, nor is he able to justify large-scale combat actions to the strategic actors. The pressures exerted by the strategic actors serve to limit his flexibility in employing the elements of operational art (Figure 11).

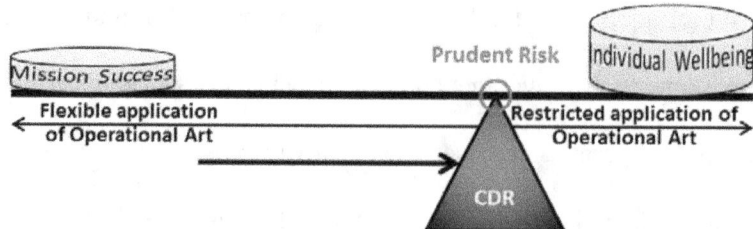

T$_4$ (August 2003 through June 2004) = Stability operations – risk is re-balanced with less options available and a restriction in applying operational art with less willingness to accept casualties, public support for offensive operations is waning, consensus within the Executive and Legislative Branches still exists but is waning, and mass media less supportive of the effort. *Examples of military actions: Presence patrols, political development, infrastructure development and reconstruction, and host nation security force development*

Figure 11: Time Four (T$_4$).

*Source:* Created by the author.

Instead of focusing on the vast array of options to accomplish a given task, he must consider the strategic actors in his calculus. He and his staff possess the necessary training to deal with a myriad of factors relating to risk from the enemy and environment, but are limited in their exposure on how to best calculate the pressures applied by the strategic actors. The commander may possess some degree of intuition as to how he must deal with these actors, more than likely it is second-hand and most definitely not formal. When he and his staff turn to doctrine for advice and guidance to deal with the added pressure, the doctrine does not address how to rebalance his risk equation from the force generated by the strategic actors. This leads to decisions that are restricting, safe, less aggressive, focused on the preservation of soldiers, and not necessarily focused on linking tactical actions to strategic objectives in time, space, and purpose. This case, as with the previous cases, lends evidence to the model developed and presented in this study.

66

## CONCLUSION

The 2012 edition of the Army Doctrine Reference Publication 5-0 *The Operations Process* widely disseminated and described as the Army's "common frame of reference and language that commanders and staffs use for the exercise of mission command," dedicates 161 words to explain risk, which seems entirely miniscule when whole operations hinge on mitigating risk.[129] Joint Publication 5-0 *Joint Operation Planning* describes that "determining the risk is more an art than a science" which suggests using some degree of intuition, experience, and judgment when identifying the level and degree of risk to an operation.[130] U.S. military doctrine inadequately teaches, guides, and advises commanders on the topic of risk in terms of both the mission and the individual soldier. The model developed within this study suggests the plausibility that individuals are increasing in strategic importance in modern warfare. The model is plausible because current military doctrine does little to prepare commanders and staffs to mitigate risks through application of operational art when external actors play such a critical role in applying pressure in the risk equation.

An extensive literature review, exposing the reader to several key definitions central to the argument and a detailed discussion of formal works on risk, casualty aversion, the CNN effect, and Warrior Ethos proved most critical to this study. This monograph defined critical concepts of the individual, risk as described at the national level through Army level, the definition of modern warfare, strategy, and operational art, all imperative to the study. Grounded in key concepts, this monograph analyzed writings on risk at multiple echelons within the United States' military framework, casualty aversion literature as it relates to public support, the importance of mass media to the support for war, and Warrior Ethos as it affects civilians and

---

[129] U.S. Department of the Army, Army Doctrine Reference Publication 5-0, iii, 1–12.

[130] U.S. Joint Chiefs of Staff, Joint Publication 5-0, IV–11.

military alike. The methodology section of the monograph took these concepts and built a model on their foundation to explain the dynamics of risk when external forces apply pressure on the commander's risk decision.

This section discusses a model developed by the author that speaks to the balance a commander must strike between mission success and protection of the soldier and where that balance exists is where the commander accepts risk to both the mission and the soldier. The methodology used in this study was a plausibility probe, which allowed the author to evaluate the developed model in terms of potential validity and value in further analysis.[131] This monograph introduced actors external to the commander that profoundly affects his risk balance. Plausibly, these actors, in combination or individually, exert pressure on the commander as he develops and reacts to mission orders or changes in his operational environment. The monograph showed that depending on where and how much pressure these actors apply determines if the commander has more options, or less, and the correlating increased, or decreased flexibility in how he applies the elements of operational art to achieve the desired strategic end state. The plausibility probe methodology allowed the author to show the model has logical merit and requires further study. Analyzing case studies based on this model help show plausibility in the next section.

The case study section established time as a foundation and that it is broken in sections overlaid against the model. Framing these five case studies are the Bush administration's initial discussion to go to war in Iraq, circa September 2002, and the transition of sovereignty to the Iraqi government in June 2004. Each of the times, when evaluated against the variables of casualty aversion, public support, political consensus, and mass media position, showed plausibility of the model. Each case study remained structurally similar, starting with an introductory reference for that period followed with analysis concerning the four critical

---

[131] Eckstein, *Regarding Politics*, 147.

68

variables. Summarily, the model is both plausible and logic in structure and validity. As with every model, there will be detractors.

The author believes that the main arguments against this model and that doctrine is insufficient in providing parameters for risk are that commanders mitigate risk intuitively and that the proposed model may only have merit with the Iraq case. Some may argue that commanders and their staffs account for risks intuitively. Somewhere in their experience and schooling, they gained enough understanding to account for risk in operations. Commanders have dealt with the fog of war and risk for centuries without any more doctrine than exists today, much less in fact. They possess experience with these decisions and therefor can think through the risk equation without further input. That argument has foundation, and is well beyond the scope of this monograph. However, one could argue that commanders have been executing leadership for centuries, but the U.S. Army felt it necessary to publish 100 pages codifying leadership guidance in Army Doctrine Reference Publication 6-22 *Army Leadership*. Perhaps, it would be worth the effort to better articulate risk so our commanders and staffs had a similar foundation as with leadership. The second argument may hold that this monograph is very narrow in application that it may only apply to the first few years of the war in Iraq. Again, this is far beyond the scope of this monograph. However, in a general look back in history, Vietnam showed similar linkages that strategic actors had a profound effect on the war effort and the subsequent views on risk to mission or soldier. Clearly, these arguments opposing this monograph have merit, addressing them with further scholarship may prove helpful.

The research and study for this monograph leads the author to propose three recommendations. The first is to continue the model with an additional step. The data compiled shows a potential next step in the model building from $T_4$ (Figure 11), one that shows the executive wishing a return to the kinetic mission oriented task of defeating a rising insurgency with the remaining three strategic actors continuing to press for the wellbeing of the service member. On the face of it, the actors appear to press on both mission and individual wellbeing when the commander remains in the more restrictive position addressed above in $T_4$. It would appear that the commander would again have to adjust his risk equation to account for the added pressure on the mission, but not to such a degree, that he ignores the pressure placed on individual wellbeing. Figure 12 depicts what this time period might look like with further analysis of the data.

$T_5$ (July 2004 through January 2006) = Rise of the insurgency and civil war – risk is teetering on out of balance with renewed emphasis on offensive operations (risk of mission failure), but less willingness to accept casualties, public support is waning, consensus within the Executive and Legislative Branches lessening, and mass media is less supportive of the effort. *Examples of military actions: Major offensive operations in insurgent strongholds (Fallujah), preponderance of attacks on US forces, increasing casualties; continued presence patrols, political development, infrastructure development and reconstruction, and host nation security force development*

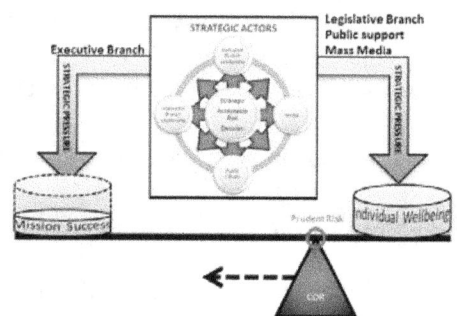

Figure 12: Time Five ($T_5$).

*Source:* Created by the author.

The characterization of this period centers on the clear deviation between the Executive Branch and Legislative Branch, with the remaining strategic actors continuing to weaken support for the war effort.

The second recommendation is that Joint and Army doctrine must address the shortfall in risk understanding and strive to bridge the gap between the modern innovative qualities of doctrinal publications in the 3-0 and 5-0 categories and the antiquated doctrine that poorly addresses tactical risk. The final recommendation is that the Army must better educate commanders and staffs about risk. Specifically, the impacts strategic actors place on their risk calculation. As risk is an important part of operational design and operational art, a comprehensive review of risk in a similar fashion as the reviews conducted for mission

70

command, operational art, and leadership would fully support the operational design

methodology and empower commanders and staffs with the right understanding to add a needed

dose of science with the art.

## APPENDIX A: GRAPHICS REFLECTING POLLING DATA

Appendix A consists of a series of graphs that depict polling data relevant to the study over time. Each graph compiles raw polling data derived from multiple sources available from the non-partisan website, PollingReport.com.

### Graphic 1

The first graphic depicts answers to the general polling question "Do you think going to war with Iraq was the right decision?" This question is an amalgamation of similar questions asked throughout different polling organizations. There were several variations of this question asked over time with answers ranging from "favor" or "oppose", "correct" or "mistake", "support" or "oppose", and "should have" or "should not have", and "unsure" for those that have neither a favorable nor negative feeling about the decision. The author depicts each of these answers over time with a trend line to illustrate the nature of respondent's feelings about the questions. Underpinning the graphic is the monthly hostile death toll for U.S. service persons in Iraq. The final aspect of the graphic is the overlay of significant events in or pertaining to the war in Iraq for the period of the study.

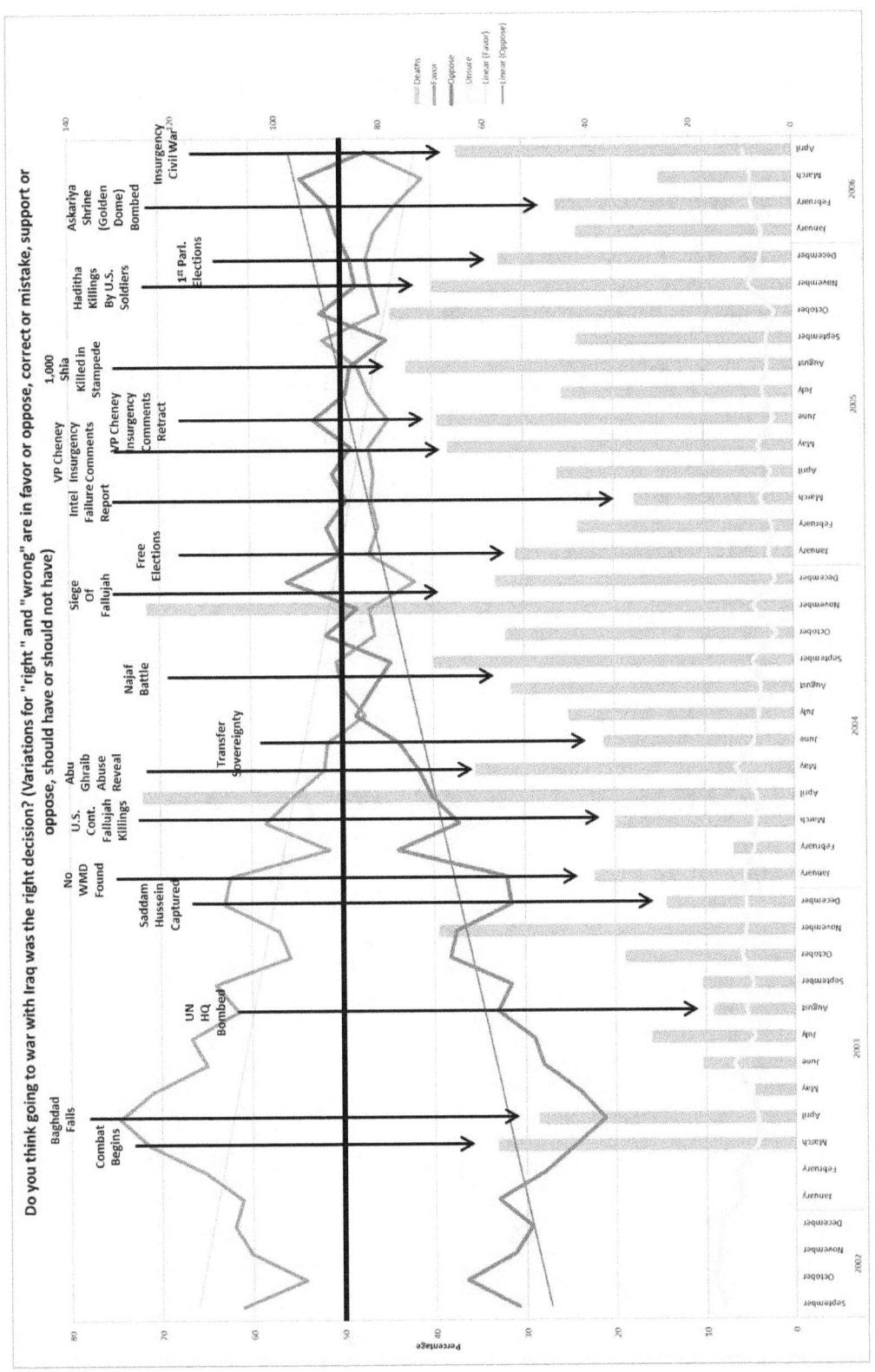

Graphic 1: "Do you think going to war with Iraq was the right decision?"

## Graphic 2

The second graphic depicts answers to the general polling question "Do you think the costs of war are worth it?" This question is an amalgamation of similar questions asked throughout different polling organizations. There were several variations of this question asked over time with references to cost ranging from "casualties," "expense in treasure," "national prestige" or "morality" and "unsure" for those that have neither a favorable nor negative feeling about the cost. The author depicts each of these answers over time with a trend line to illustrate the nature of respondent's feelings about the questions. Underpinning the graphic is the monthly hostile death toll for U.S. service members in Iraq. The final aspect of the graphic is the overlay of significant events in or pertaining to the war in Iraq for the period of the study.

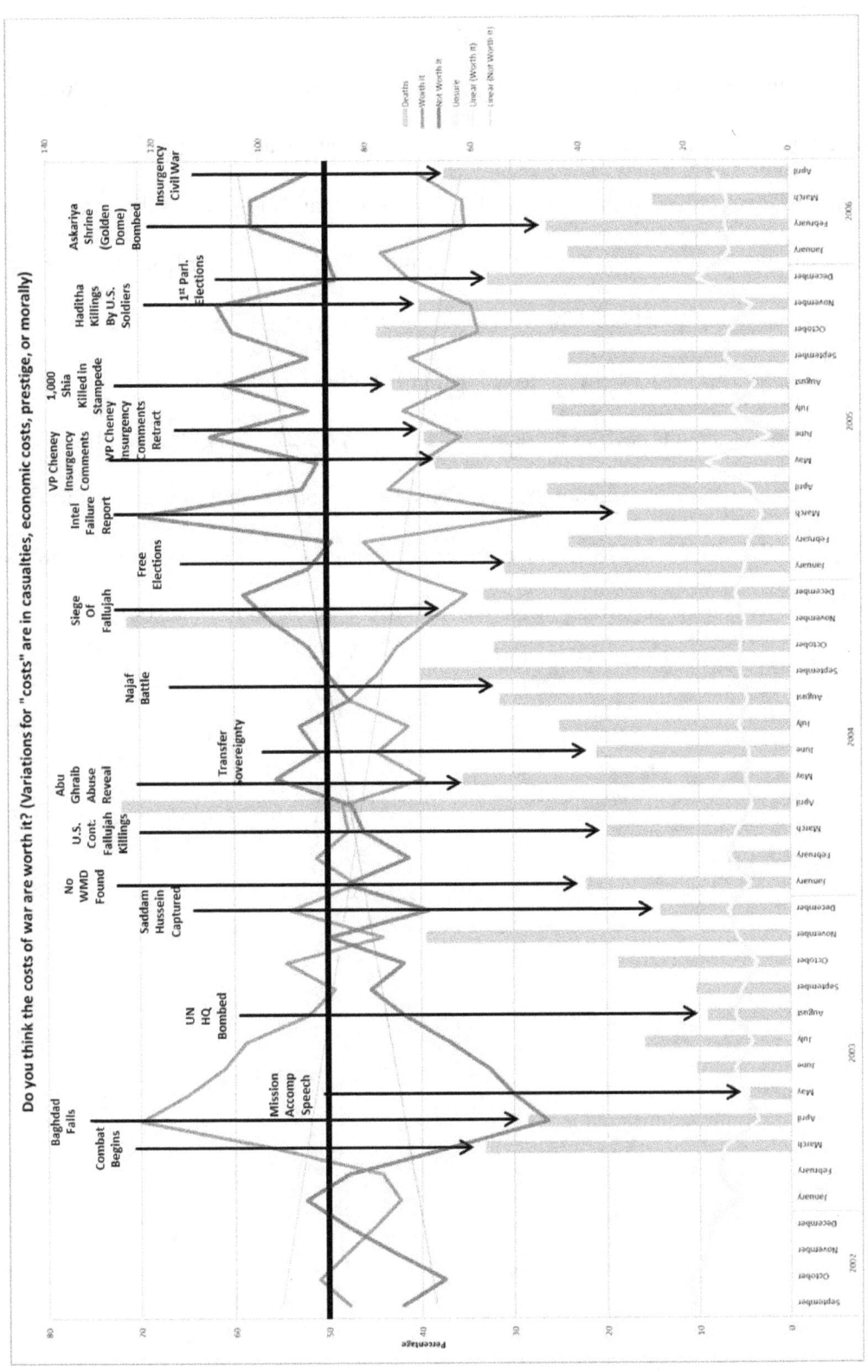

Graphic 2: "Do you think the costs of war are worth it?"

## Graphic 3

The third graphic depicts answers to the general polling question "Do you think the U.S. is succeeding or winning the war?" This question is an amalgamation of similar questions asked throughout different polling organizations. There were several variations of this question asked over time with references to "succeeding" and "winning." These ranging from terms of making progress, an improving situation, achieving goals, and plan is apparent and succeeding and "unsure" for those that have neither a favorable nor negative feeling about succeeding or winning the war. The author depicts each of these answers over time with a trend line to illustrate the nature of respondent's feelings about the questions. Underpinning the graphic is the monthly hostile death toll for U.S. service members in Iraq. The final aspect of the graphic is the overlay of significant events in or pertaining to the war in Iraq for the period of the study.

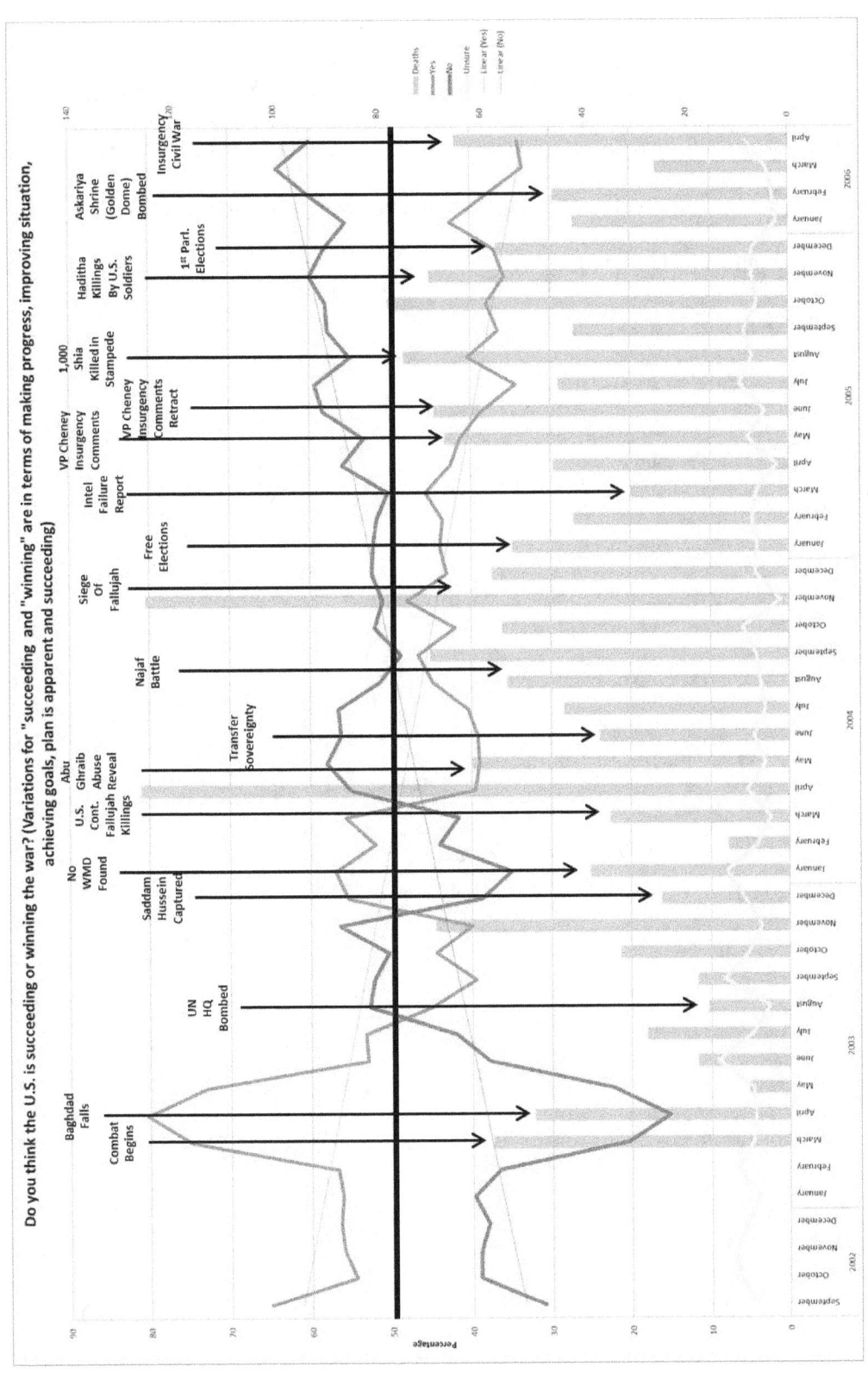

Graphic 3: "Do you think the U.S. is succeeding or winning the war?"

77

<u>Graphic 4</u>

The fourth graphic depicts United States combat deaths beginning with the outbreak of war through April 2006. The line graph depicts the numbers of combat deaths each month for the period. The area chart depicts the aggregated numbers of combat deaths for the period. The final aspect of the graphic is the overlay of significant events in or pertaining to the war in Iraq for the period of the study.

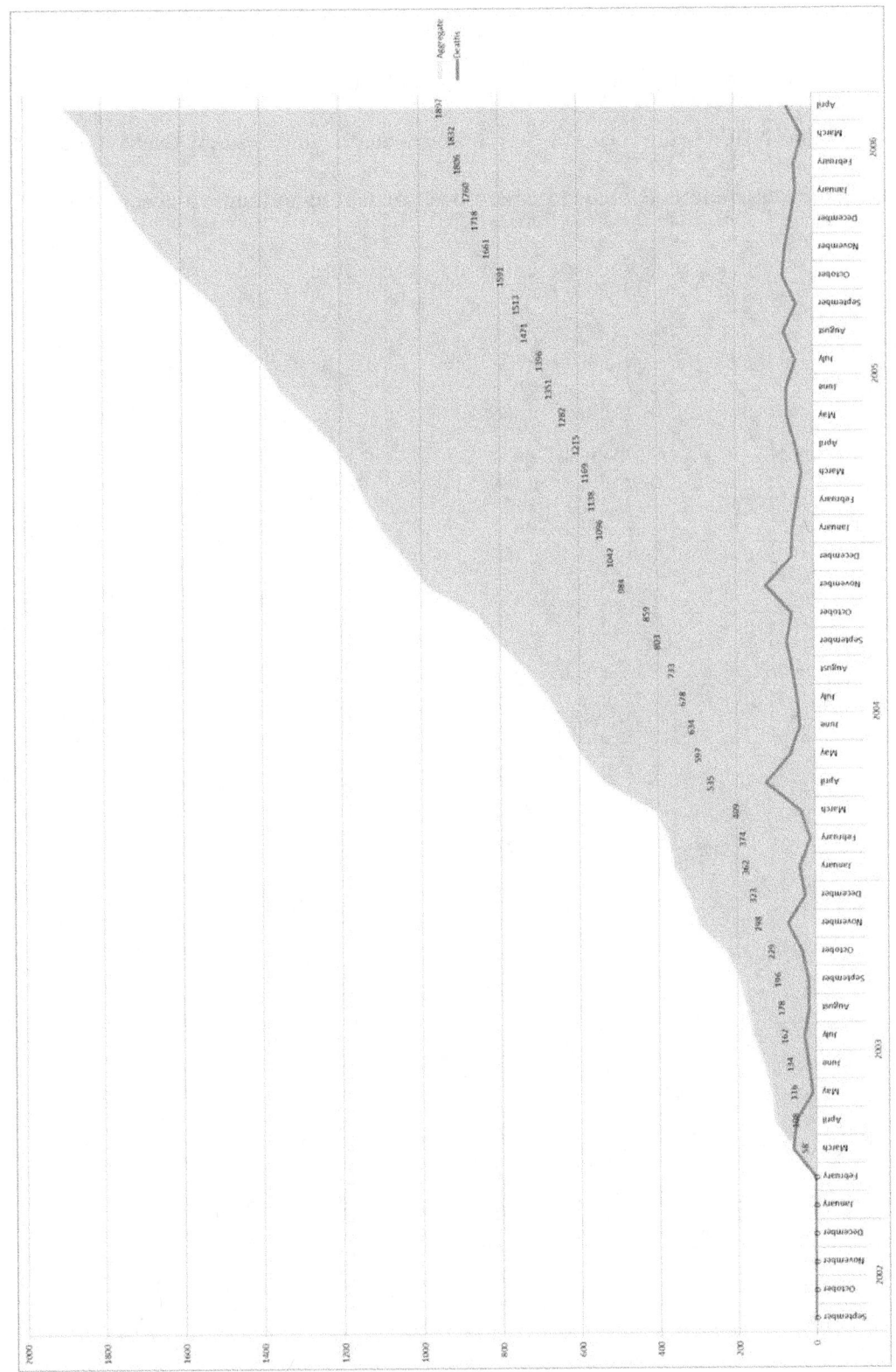

Graphic 4: U.S. combat deaths monthly and aggregated for the period of study.

<u>Graphic 5</u>

The fifth graphic depicts the minutes devoted by the major broadcast news organizations (ABC, CBS, and NBC) to the war. The two measures are the minutes devoted to combat actions in Iraq and the total minutes devoted to other stories pertaining to Iraq in a general sense.

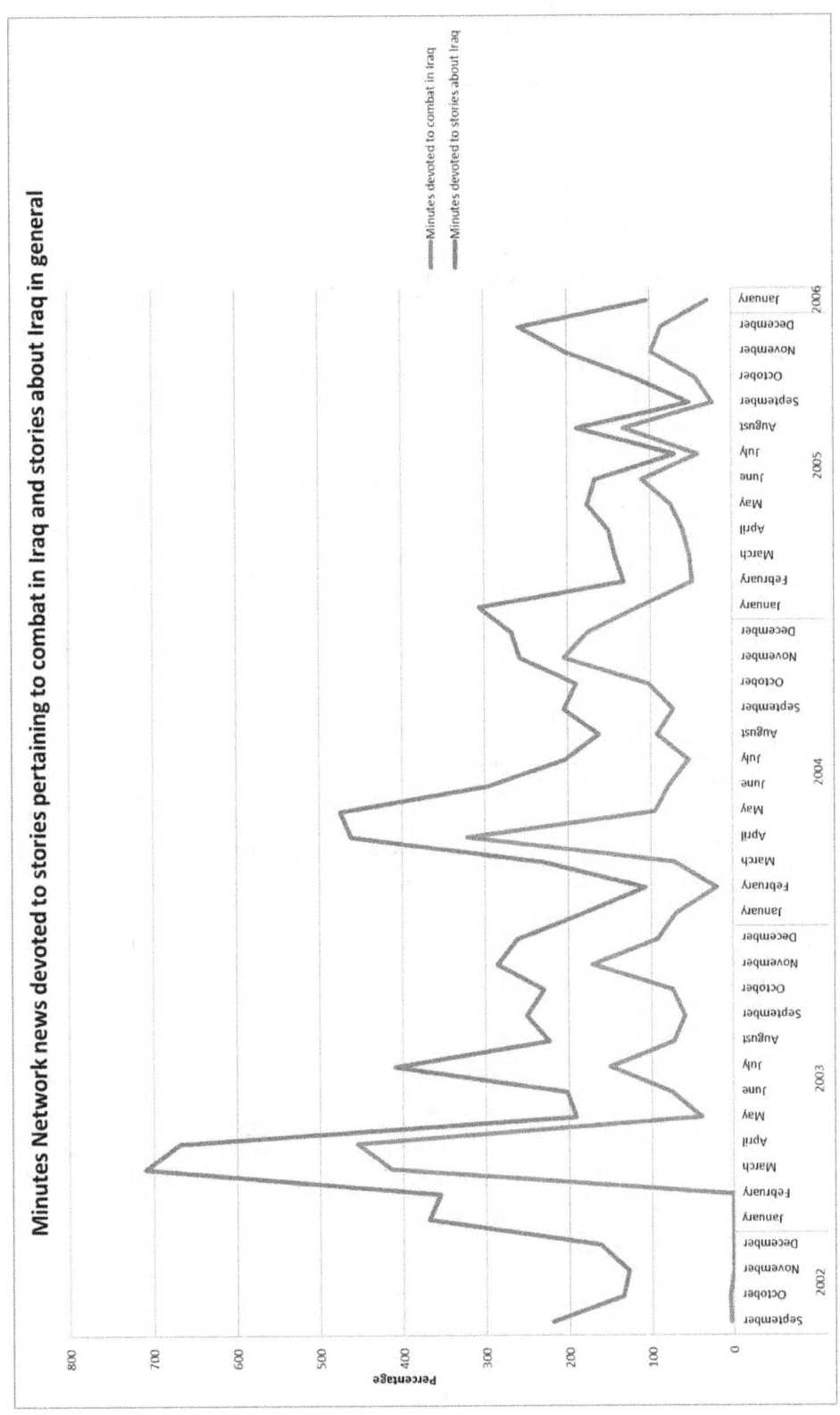

Graphic 5: Minutes network news (ABC, CBS, and NBC) devoted to stories pertaining to combat in Iraq and stories about Iraq in general.

81

The fifth series of graphics depict various relevant questions specific to a particular case study.

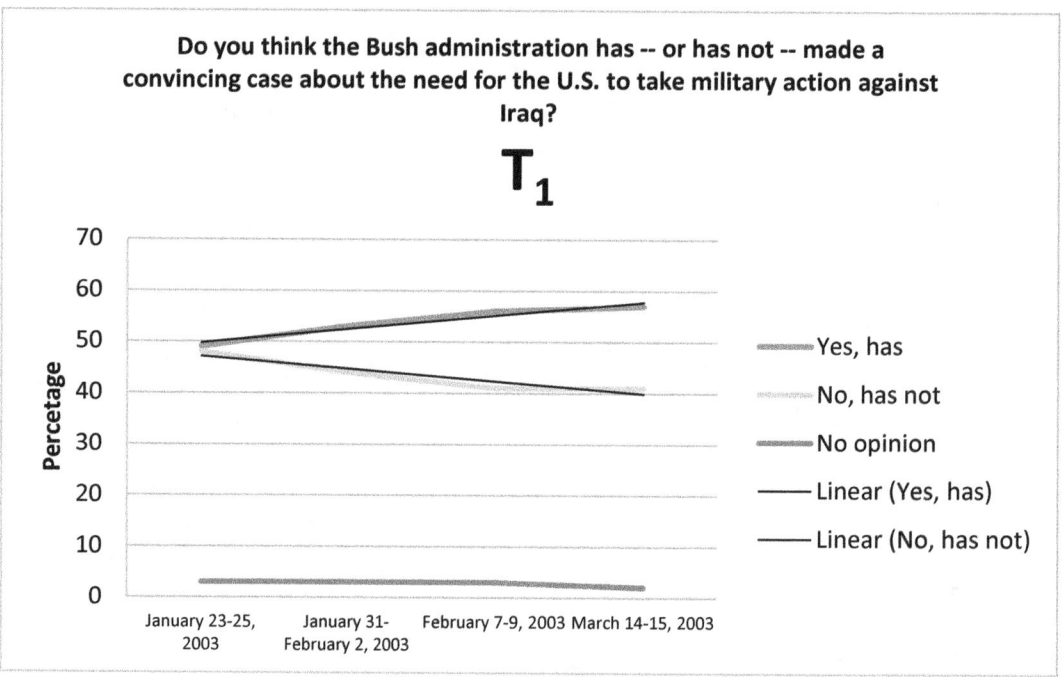

Graphic 6A: Graphical representation of a Gallup Poll conducted March 14-15, 2003. The sample was 519 adults nationwide with a margin of error of ±3 percent.[132]

_____

[132] Jones, "Gallup Poll."

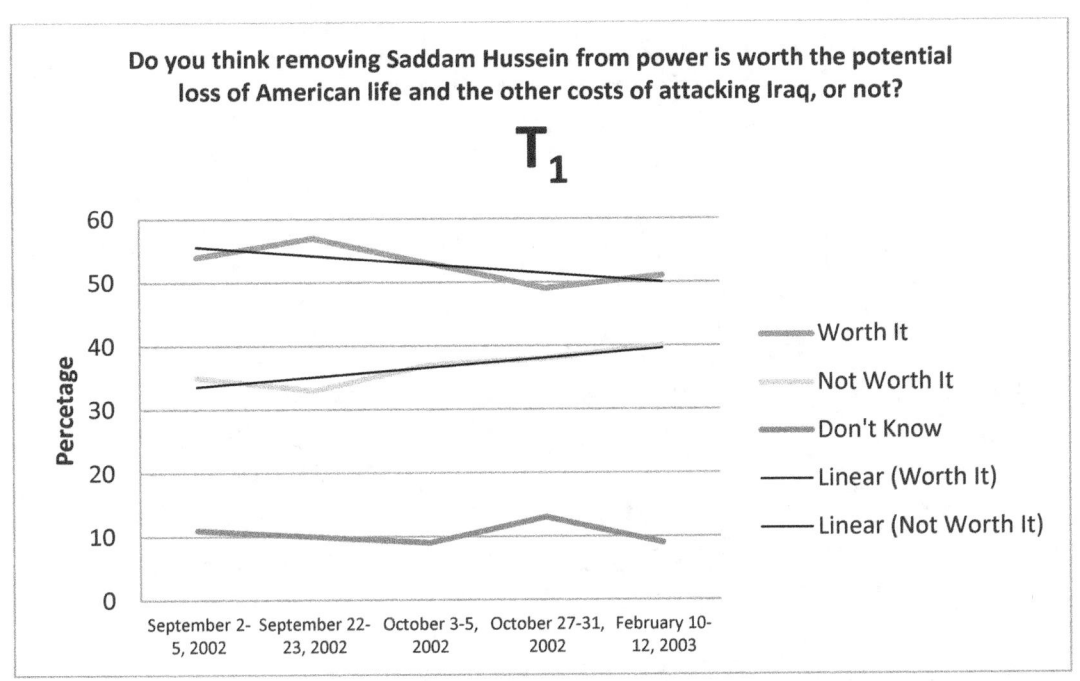

Graphic 6B: Graphical representation of a CBS News Poll conducted March 26-27, 2003 with data portrayed for the ($T_1$) period. The sample was **868** adults nationwide with a margin of error of ±3 percent.

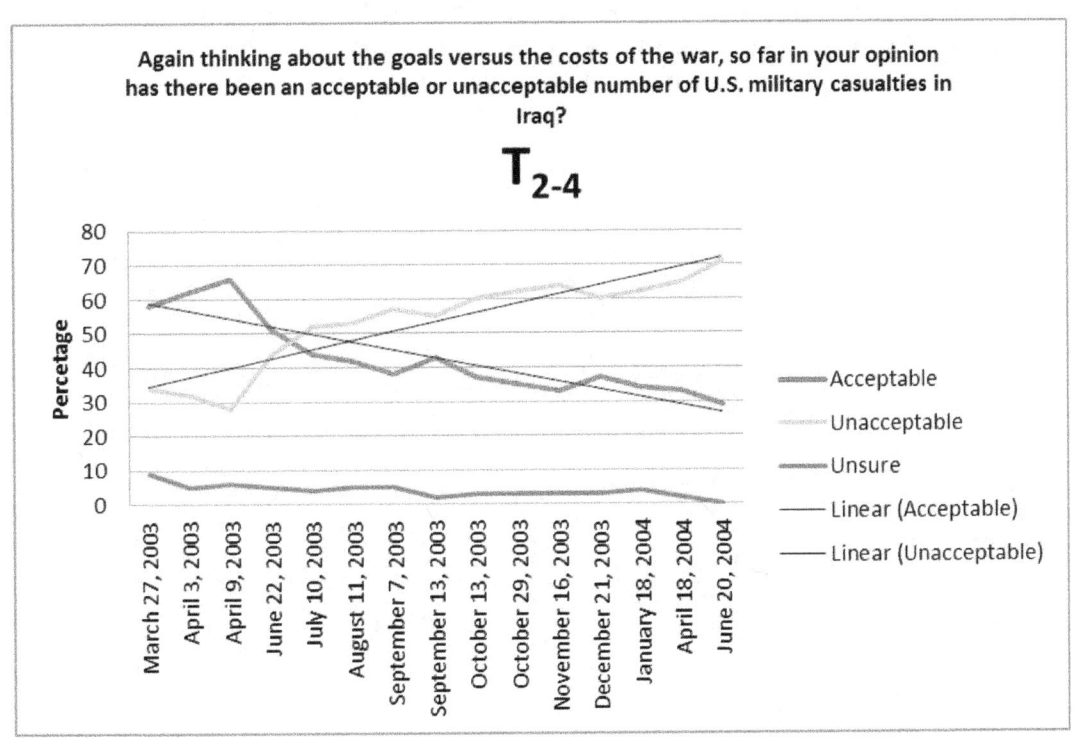

Graphic 6C: Graphical representation of a ABC News/Washington Post Poll conducted through May 11-15, 2006 with data portrayed for the ($T_2 - T_4$) periods. The sample was 1,103 adults nationwide with a margin of error of ± 3 percent.

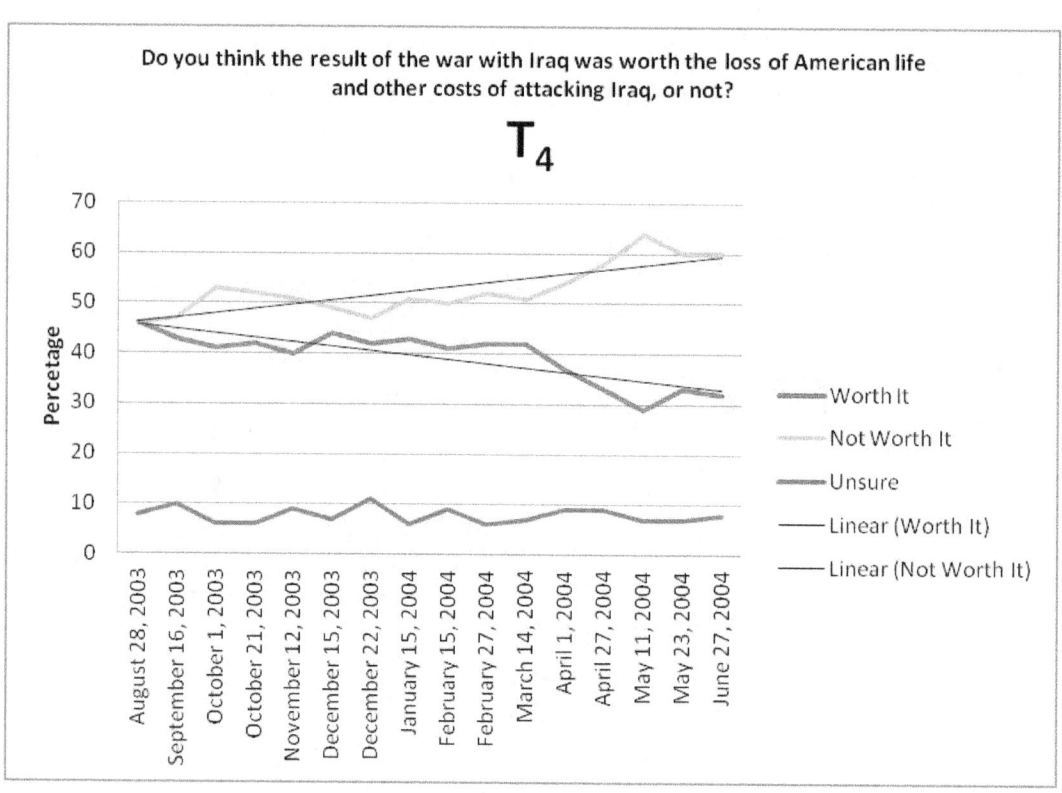

Graphic 6D: Graphical representation of a CBS News/New York Times Poll conducted through July 21-25, 2006 with data portrayed for the $T_4$ period. The sample was 1,127 adults nationwide with a margin of error of ± 3 percent.

APPENDIX B: HISTORICAL DOCTRINAL REFERENCES TO RISK AND MITIGATION

This appendix highlights risk data from Field Manual 3-0 (2001), Field Manual 3-0 (2008), Army Doctrine Reference Publication 3-0 (2012), Field Manual 5-0 (2005), and Army Doctrinal Reference Publication 5-0 (2012) to illustrate the lack of maturation risk enjoyed in doctrine until 2012. Until Army Doctrinal Reference Publication 5-0 (2012), risk transited eleven years with barely a word change. With the publishing of Army Doctrinal Reference Publication 5-0, risk received an update. However, the doctrine still failed to address the risk hazards that the commander must understand, but may not control, the impacts from strategic actors.

Risk in FM 3-0 dated February 2001:

6-100. Risk, uncertainty, and chance are inherent in all military operations. When commanders accept risk, they create opportunities to seize, retain, and exploit the initiative and achieve decisive results. Risk is a potent catalyst that fuels opportunity. The willingness to incur operational risk is often the key to exposing enemy weaknesses that the enemy considers beyond friendly reach. Understanding risk requires calculated assessments coupled with boldness and imagination. Successful commanders assess risk continuously throughout operations and mitigate it through creative operational design.

6-101. It is reckless to commit forces without adequate planning and preparation. It is equally rash to delay action while waiting for perfect intelligence and synchronization. Reasonably estimating and intentionally accepting risk is fundamental to conducting operations. It is essential to successful battle command. Successfully applying military force requires commanders who assess the risks, analyze and minimize the hazards, and execute a plan that accounts for those hazards. Experienced commanders balance audacity and imagination with risk and uncertainty to strike at a time and place and in a manner wholly unexpected by enemy forces. This is the essence of surprise. It results from carefully considering and accepting risk. (FMs 3-90 and 6-0 discuss tactical risk.)

6-102. Operational art balances risk and opportunity to create and maintain the conditions necessary to seize, retain, and exploit the initiative and achieve decisive results. During execution, opportunity is fleeting. The surest means to create opportunity is to accept risk while minimizing hazards to friendly forces. A good operational design considers risk and uncertainty equally with friction and chance. The final plans and orders then provide the flexibility commanders need to take advantage of opportunity in complex, dynamic environments.

## Risk in FM 3-0 dated February 2008:

6-100. Risk, uncertainty, and chance are inherent in all military operations. When commanders accept risk, they create opportunities to seize, retain, and exploit the initiative and achieve decisive results. Risk is a potent catalyst that fuels opportunity. The willingness to incur operational risk is often the key to exposing enemy weaknesses that the enemy considers beyond friendly reach. Understanding risk requires calculated assessments coupled with boldness and imagination. Successful commanders assess risk continuously throughout operations and mitigate it through creative operational design.

6-101. It is reckless to commit forces without adequate planning and preparation. It is equally rash to delay action while waiting for perfect intelligence and synchronization. Reasonably estimating and intentionally accepting risk is fundamental to conducting operations. It is essential to successful battle command. Successfully applying military force requires commanders who assess the risks, analyze and minimize the hazards, and execute a plan that accounts for those hazards. Experienced commanders balance audacity and imagination with risk and uncertainty to strike at a time and place and in a manner wholly unexpected by enemy forces. This is the essence of surprise. It results from carefully considering and accepting risk. (FMs 3-90 and 6-0 discuss tactical risk.)

6-102. Operational art balances risk and opportunity to create and maintain the conditions necessary to seize, retain, and exploit the initiative and achieve decisive results. During execution, opportunity is fleeting. The surest means to create opportunity is to accept risk while minimizing hazards to friendly forces. A good operational design considers risk and uncertainty equally with friction and chance. The final plans and orders then provide the flexibility commanders need to take advantage of opportunity in complex, dynamic environments.

<u>Risk in ADRP 3-0 dated May 2012:</u>

4-51. Risk, uncertainty, and chance are inherent in all military operations. When commanders accept risk, they create opportunities to seize, retain, and exploit the initiative and achieve decisive results. The willingness to incur risk is often the key to exposing enemy weaknesses that the enemy considers beyond friendly reach. Understanding risk requires assessments coupled with boldness and imagination. Successful commanders assess and mitigate risk continuously throughout the operations process.

4-52. Inadequate planning and preparation recklessly risks forces. It is equally rash to delay action while waiting for perfect intelligence and synchronization. Reasonably estimating and intentionally accepting risk is fundamental to conducting operations and essential to mission command. Experienced commanders balance audacity and imagination with risk and uncertainty to strike at a time and place and in a manner wholly unexpected by enemy forces. This is the essence of surprise. It results from carefully considering and accepting risk.

4-53. Commanders accept risk and seek opportunity to create and maintain the conditions necessary to seize, retain, and exploit the initiative and achieve decisive results. During execution, opportunity is fleeting. The surest means to create opportunity is to accept risk while minimizing hazards to friendly forces. A good operational approach considers risk and uncertainty equally with friction and chance. The final plans and orders then provide the flexibility commanders need to take advantage of opportunity in a highly competitive and dynamic environment.

## Risk in FM 5-0 dated January 2005:

1-72. Uncertainty and risk are inherent in tactical operations. Commanders cannot be successful without the capability of acting under conditions of uncertainty while balancing various risks and taking advantage of opportunities. Planning helps commanders reduce uncertainty and risk. It is a risk management tool.

1-73. During planning, commanders and staffs perform risk management (see FM 100-14). They identify potential hazards to mission accomplishment and assess the probability and severity of each hazard. Commanders determine the acceptable level of risk and express this determination in their planning guidance. The staff uses the commander's risk guidance as a guide for developing control measures to reduce identified hazards and for developing branches. Risk guidance is also incorporated into each COA developed, and in turn, each COA considered is evaluated by its acceptability. (Acceptability is the degree to which the tactical advantage gained by executing the COA justifies the cost in resources, especially casualties.)

1-74. Because uncertainty exists in all military operations, every military decision incurs some risk. In designing plans, the commander decides how much risk to accept. Figure 1-5, shows several adjustments available to reduce the risk associated in a specific operation. Incorporating risk reduction measures adds to the plan's flexibility during execution.

1-75. Risk reduction does not always mean increasing knowledge of the enemy at the expense of time. A flexible plan can partially compensate for a lack of intelligence. Unclear situations may require increasing the depth of the security area, size and number of security units, or size of the reserve. Combat and movement formations that provide for initial enemy contact with the smallest possible friendly force may also be appropriate. Another way to compensate for increased risk is to allocate time and resources for developing the situation to subordinate elements.

<u>Risk in ADRP 5-0 dated May 2012:</u>

1-55. *Risk management* is the process of identifying, assessing, and controlling risks arising from operational factors and making decisions that balance risk cost with mission benefits (JP 3-0). Identifying and accepting prudent risk is a principle of mission command. Throughout the operations process, commanders and staffs use risk management to identify and mitigate risks associated with all hazards that have the potential to injure or kill friendly and civilian personnel, damage or destroy equipment, or otherwise impact mission effectiveness. Like targeting, risk management begins in planning and continues through preparation and execution. Risk management consists of the following steps:

- Identify hazards.
- Assess hazards to determine risks.
- Develop controls and make risk decisions.
- Implement controls.
- Supervise and evaluate.

1-56. All staff elements incorporate risk management into their running estimates and provide recommendations for control measures to mitigate risk within their areas of expertise. Risk management integration during all operations process activities is the primary responsibility of the unit's protection officer or the operations officer.

Accept Prudent Risk to Exploit Opportunities

4-6. Uncertainty and risk are inherent in all military operations. Successful commanders are comfortable operating under conditions of uncertainty, as they balance various risks and take advantage of opportunities. Opportunities are events that offer better ways to succeed. Commanders recognize opportunities by continuously monitoring and evaluating the situation. Failure to understand the opportunities inherent in an enemy's action surrenders the initiative. Most opportunities are fleeting. When they present themselves, commanders usually have only a short window of time in which to act. In operations, it is better to err on the side of speed, audacity, and momentum than on the side of caution, all else being equal. Bold decisions give the best promise of success; however, when acting on an opportunity, commanders must consider the difference between a prudent risk and a gamble.

4-7. *Prudent risk* is a deliberate exposure to potential injury or loss when the commander judges the outcome in terms of mission accomplishment as worth the cost (ADP 6-0). Reasonably estimating and intentionally accepting risk is not gambling. Gambling, in contrast to prudent risk taking, is staking the success of an entire action on a single event without considering the hazard to the force should the event not unfold as envisioned. Therefore, commanders avoid taking gambles. Commanders carefully determine risks, analyze and minimize as many hazards as possible, and then take prudent risks to exploit opportunities.

4-8. Because uncertainty exists in all military operations, every military decision contains risk. Commanders exercise the art of command when deciding how much risk to accept. As shown in figure 4-1, the commander has several techniques available to reduce the risk associated in a specific operation. Some of these techniques for reducing risk take resources from the decisive operation, which reduces the concentration of effects at the decisive point.

4-9. The commander has the option to redirect the efforts of forces previously used to reduce risk toward strengthening the force's decisive operation as more information becomes available. In any operation, the relationship between information, uncertainty, risk, size of reserves and security forces, and the disposition of the main body may change frequently. The commander must continually weigh this balance and make adjustments as needed.

4-10. These adjustments can create problems. Too many changes or changes made too rapidly in task organization, mission, and priorities can have negative effects on the operations process. For example, if a commander changes task organization too frequently, the force fails to develop the flexibility provided by teamwork. On the other hand, if the commander fails to change the task organization when dictated by circumstances, the force lacks flexibility to adapt to those changing circumstances. It is then unable to react effectively to enemy moves or act with the concentration of effects that lead to mission success. (See FM 3-90 for a detailed discussion of the art of tactics and risk reduction.)

BIBLIOGRAPHY

Bartholomees, J. Boone, and Army War College (U.S.). Strategic Studies Institute. *U.S. Army War College Guide to National Security Issues*. Carlisle, Pa.: Strategic Studies Institute, U.S. Army War College, 2008. http://purl.access.gpo.gov/GPO/LPS95737 (accessed November 6, 2012).

Bishop, Timothy F., and Army War College (U.S.). *A Nation At War: Combat Casualties and Public Support*. USAWC strategy research project. Carlisle Barracks, Pa: U.S. Army War College, 2008. http://handle.dtic.mil/100.2/ADA478483 (accessed November 8, 2012).

Brown, John S. *Kevlar Legions : The Transformation of The U.S. Army, 1989-2005*. Washington, D.C.: Center of Military History United States Army, 2011. http://purl.fdlp.gov/GPO/gpo16049 (accessed November 6, 2012).

Bush, George W. *Decision Points*. New York: Crown Publishers, 2010.

————. "President Declares End to Major Combat in Iraq." *CBS News*, n.d. http://www.cbsnews.com/8301-500257_162-551946.html (accessed November 22, 2012).

Clausewitz, Carl von. *On War*. Edited by Michael Howard and Peter Paret. Princeton, N.J.: Princeton University Press, 1984.

Coker, Christopher. *The Warrior Ethos: Military Culture and the War on Terror*. London; New York: Routledge, 2007.

Dobbins, James, Seth G. Jones, Benjamin Runkle, and Siddharth Mohandas. *Occupying Iraq: a History of the Coalition Provisional Authority*. Santa Monica, CA: RAND Corp, 2009.

Dolman, Everett C. *Pure Strategy: Power and Principle in the Space and Information Age*. London; New York: Frank Cass, 2005.

Eckstein, Harry. *Regarding Politics: Essays on Political Theory, Stability, and Change*. Berkeley: University of California Press, 1992.

Epstein, Robert M. *Napoleon's Last Victory and the Emergence of Modern War*. Lawrence, Kan.: University Press of Kansas, 1994.

Franks, Tommy. "General Tommy Franks." Radio, March 27, 2003. http://www.freerepublic.com/focus/f-news/878280/posts (accessed January 12, 2012).

Gelpi, Christopher, Peter D. Feaver, and Jason Reifler. "Success Matters: Casualty Sensitivity and the War in Iraq." *International Security* 30, no. 3 (December 1, 2005): 7–46. http://www.jstor.org/stable/4137486 (accessed December 3, 2012).

Gilboa, Eytan. "Global Television News and Foreign Policy: Debating the CNN Effect." *International Studies Perspectives* 6, no. 3 (August 2005): 325–341. http://doi.wiley.com/10.1111/j.1528-3577.2005.00211.x (accessed November 16, 2012).

Greenblatt, Alan. *Media Bias: Are the Major Sources of News Trustworthy?* The CQ Researcher

Online Volume Number 14., Issue Number (October 14, 2004, n.d. http://library.cqpress.com/cqresearcher/cqresrre2004101500 (accessed January 12, 2013).

Jones, Jeffrey M. "Public Support for Iraq Invasion Inches Upward." *Gallup*, March 17, 2003. http://www.gallup.com/poll/7990/Public-Support-Iraq-Invasion-Inches-Upward.aspx (accessed December 4, 2012).

Kasupski, III., Bernard W. "CNN Effect: A Direct Path to the American Center of Gravity?" Newport, Rhode Island: U.S. Naval War College, 2000.

Lacquement, Jr., Richard A. "The Casualty-Aversion Myth." *Naval War College Review* 57, no. 1 (Winter 2004): 39–57.

Lichter, S. Robert, and Linda S. Lichter. "Media Monitor: 2003 Year in Review." *CMPA: Center for Media and Public Affairs*, February 2004. http://www.cmpa.com/files/media_monitor/04janfeb.pdf (accessed January 16, 2013).

———. "Media Monitor: 2004 Year in Review." *CMPA: Center for Media and Public Affairs*, February 2005. http://www.cmpa.com/files/media_monitor/05janfeb.pdf (accessed January 16, 2013).

———. "Media Monitor: George Bush's Postwar Blues TV News Coverage of President Bush Since the Iraq War." *CMPA: Center for Media and Public Affairs*, December 2003. http://www.cmpa.com/files/media_monitor/03novdec.pdf (accessed January 16, 2013).

———. "Media Monitor: The Media Go to War TV News Coverage of the War in Iraq." *CMPA: Center for Media and Public Affairs*, August 2003. http://www.cmpa.com/files/media_monitor/03novdec.pdf (accessed January 16, 2013).

Liddell Hart, Basil Henry. *Strategy*. New York, N.Y., U.S.A.: Meridian, 1991.

McHugh, John M., and Raymond T. Odierno. "2012 U.S. Army Posture Statement." *U.S. Department of the Army*, February 17, 2012. https://secureweb2.hqda.pentagon.mil/VDAS_ArmyPostureStatement/2012/ (accessed November 16, 2012).

Newport, Frank, David W. Moore, and Jeffrey M. Jones. "Special Release: American Opinion on the War." *Gallup*, March 21, 2003. http://www.gallup.com/poll/8068/Special-Release-American-Opinion-War.aspx (accessed December 5, 2012).

PollingReport.com. "Iraq." *PollingReport.com*, n.d. http://www.pollingreport.com/iraq.htm (accessed December 4, 2012).

Project Vote Smart. "'Iraq' 2002 National Key Votes." *Project Vote Smart*, n.d. https://votesmart.org/bills/NA/2002/?state=NA&category=&year=2002&search=iraq#.U L6fMIZCN8H (accessed December 5, 2012).

———. "'Iraq' 2003 National Key Votes." *Project Vote Smart*, n.d. https://votesmart.org/bills/NA/2003/?state=NA&category=&year=2003&search=iraq#.U L6hK4ZCN8E (accessed December 5, 2012).

———. "'Iraq' 2004 National Key Votes." *Project Vote Smart*, n.d. https://votesmart.org/bills/NA/2004/?state=NA&category=&year=2003&search=iraq#.U L6hK4ZCN8E (accessed December 5, 2012).

Sanchez, Ricardo S. *Wiser in Battle: A Soldier's Story*. New York, NY: HarperCollins, 2008.

Shulimson, Jack. *U.S. Marines in Vietnam: the Landing and the Buildup, 1965*. Nashville, Tenn.: Battery Press, 1996.

Smith, S.E. "What is Mass Media?" *wiseGEEK*, n.d. http://www.wisegeek.com/what-is-mass-media.htm (accessed November 14, 2012).

Snyder, Robert L, and Everette E Dennis. *Media & Public Life*. New Brunswick [etc.]: Transaction, 1997.

Spring, Baker. "Operation Iraqi Freedom: Military Objectives Met." *The Heritage Foundation - Leadership for America*, April 18, 2003. http://www.heritage.org/research/reports/2003/04/operation-iraqi-freedom-military-objectives-met (accessed November 27, 2012).

Stech, Frank J. "Winning CNN Wars." *Parameters*, n.d. http://www.carlisle.army.mil/usawc/Parameters/Articles/1994/stech.htm (accessed November 16, 2012).

Tyndall, Andrew. "Tyndall Report monthly breakdown for yearly stories", January 11, 2013.

U.S. Department of the Army. *Composite Risk Management*. Field Manual 5-19. Washington, D.C.: U.S. Department of the Army, 2006.

———. *Hybrid Threat*. Training Circular 7-100. Washington, D.C.: U.S. Department of the Army, 2010.

———. *The Army*. Field Manual 1. Washington, D.C.: U.S. Department of the Army, 2005.

———. *The Operations Process*. Army Doctrine Reference Publication 5-0. Washington, D.C.: U.S. Department of the Army, 2012.

———. *Unified Land Operations*. Army Doctrine Publication 3-0. Washington, D.C.: U.S. Department of the Army, 2011.

———. *Unified Land Operations*. Army Doctrine Reference Publication 3-0. Washington, D.C.: U.S. Department of the Army, 2012.

U.S. Joint Chiefs of Staff. *Command and Control for Joint Land Operations*. Joint Publication 3-31. Washington, D.C.: U.S. Joint Chiefs of Staff, 2010.

———. *Department of Defense Dictionary of Military and Associated Terms*. Washington, D.C.: U.S. Joint Chiefs of Staff, 2012.

———. *Joint Operation Planning*. Joint Publication 5-0. Washington, D.C.: U.S. Joint Chiefs of Staff, 2011.

———. *Joint Operations*. Joint Publication 3-0. Washington, D.C.: U.S. Joint Chiefs of Staff, 2011.

UN Security Council. *United Nations Security Council Resolution 1441 (2002) Concerning Iraq*. S/RES/1441 (2002). UN Security Council, 2002.

Wong, Leonard, and Army War College (U.S.). Strategic Studies Institute. *Why They Fight: Combat Motivation in the Iraq War*. [Carlisle Barracks, PA]: Strategic Studies Institute, U.S. Army War College, 2003.

"Democratic Presidential Candidate's Debate." *CNN*, January 4, 2004. http://transcripts.cnn.com/TRANSCRIPTS/0401/04/se.01.html (accessed January 18, 2013).

"iCasualties | Operation Iraqi Freedom | Iraq." *Iraq Coalition Casualty Count*, n.d. http://www.icasualties.org/Iraq/index.aspx (accessed January 12, 2013).

"Watching, Reading and Listening to the News." *Pew Research Center for the People and the Press*, n.d. http://www.people-press.org/2012/09/27/section-1-watching-reading-and-listening-to-the-news-3/ (accessed December 5, 2012).